MARY WAS HERE

Where Mary Queen of Scots went
and what she did there

With a foreword by Liz Lochhead

CONTENTS

◄ A pencil portrait of Mary aged nine by
  the French court artist Francis Clouet.

FOREWORD

Mary Queen of Scots is a figure who belongs as much to myth as she does to history. Her life, and even more her death – tragic, iconic, all-but inevitable – at the hands of her cousin Elizabeth I of England are still part of the fabric of the national dream, the national trauma, here in Scotland. *'Mary Queen of Scots got her head chopped off, Mary Queen of Scots got her head chopped OFF!'* chanted the weans of my Lanarkshire primary school, on the final word flicking the yellow, curly-petalled head from a dandelion, sending it spinning across the playground. We were doing this in 1953, Coronation Year, as Elizabeth II ascended to the throne of Great Britain, and this wee rhyme with its gleefully destructive ending still echoes today from playgrounds throughout the land. 'Technically she's not actually Elizabeth II to us in Scotland. We never had an Elizabeth I here,' explained our teacher, a stickler for accuracy, as she dished out the Coronation mugs.

The romantic, anyway much romanticised, story of a beautiful red-haired woman with royal blood in her veins and a wilful and passionate nature, fated to live a tempestuous life and die a tragic death, the victim moreover of another *woman* (also royal, wilful, passionate, but clever, politic), has appealed no end to dramatists, librettists, biographers, story-tellers and audiences all over the world throughout athe centuries as much as to historians.

There have been scores and scores of historical novels, plays and operas. (Some even say 'twas the death of Darnley inspired the dark deed at Shakespeare's Elsinore which sparks off the plot of *Hamlet*.)

This beautiful, lucid and lavishly illustrated book is a wonderfully accessible and informative work for the general reader. A genuinely and properly popular history. In it are illuminated the forces – religious, political, sectarian, sexual; the figures – Knox, Darnley, Rizzio, Bothwell, Elizabeth, the cousin-she-never-met. Here are the battles, the murder, the mayhem, the mystery, the 'rape', 'the rough wooing', the kidnap, the births, the deaths, the controversies, the fashions, the progresses, the plots, the palaces and the prisons – all leading to the final scaffold and the axe. A wonderful account of the time there *were twa queens on the wan green island, and the wan green island was split intae twa kingdoms …*

Liz Lochhead
Scots Makar, or
National Poet of Scotland

Liz Lochhead is the author of Communicado Theatre Company's 1987 play *'Mary Queen of Scots Got her Head Chopped Off'*.

MARIE
REINE
ESCOS:
SE

Introduction

Mary Queen of Scots is by far the most celebrated figure in Scottish history. She is the subject of dozens of books, films and plays; she appears in hundreds of paintings; she is the subject of learned essays and doctoral theses; she is depicted on the sides of buses and on shortbread tins; her name is known throughout the world. This is quite an achievement for someone who lived 44 years, nearly half of it spent in captivity, and less than half in Scotland.

Mary's personal reign lasted less than six years. It was marked by two brutal murders, two unhappy marriages, frequent illnesses, open rebellion and civil war, and ended in defeat, imprisonment and forced abdication.

Yet for all these failings, Mary fascinates us, just as she fascinated the people of her day – whether charming them with her beauty and vivacity or appalling them with her Catholic faith and her dynastic ambitions. Her story, however brief, is bristling with intrigue and incident – and though it has been much romanticised, it has no need for embellishment. The events themselves are every bit as dramatic, surprising and tragic as the myths.

It is impossible to explore Scotland without crossing Mary's path. It almost seems as though she visited every residence, trod every byway and forded every stream. Any legend lends itself to exaggeration, but the truth is she travelled widely, and there are many places that can claim a connection with her.

This book does not set out to provide a comprehensive biography of Mary Queen of Scots. Others have performed that task with distinction. What we have tried to do is chart her progress by pinpointing specific incidents at specific places on specific dates. Some were turning points in her life; others serve to illustrate the social and political environment of the time; others are simply anecdotes from her remarkable story. We have also included sections describing her pastimes, clothing and jewellery, marriages and wider themes such as religion and health.

Some of the places Mary lived in or visited have been lost. Little remains of Fotheringhay Castle, where she was executed, and nothing at all of Kirk o' Field, where her second husband met his violent death. But fortunately many of the buildings mentioned in this book are still standing. These include her main residences at Holyrood, Stirling and Linlithgow, as well as regular retreats such as Falkland Palace and Edinburgh Castle.

In most cases, the buildings mentioned are open to the public. A directory and map are provided, to assist any reader wishing to follow in Mary's footsteps.

It was during the 1500s that portrait painting became widespread, and this presents an opportunity. The French, English and Scottish courts employed brilliant artists such as Francis Clouet, Hans Holbein and Arnold Bronckhorst, and vivid portraits of Mary and her contemporaries allow us to know how they looked – even if a court painter's skills included a talent for flattery.

Mary's career is often judged as a failure, and on the face of it that assessment is hard to refute. She was headstrong and perhaps a little vain, with a keen sense of her own importance – though these might be considered qualities essential in a monarch. She could be naïve and impetuous, sometimes ignoring good counsel or neglecting her responsibilities. Her choice of husbands could charitably be described as unwise.

But the hand she was dealt was a poor one that could not easily have been played better. Crucially, she was a Catholic woman attempting to impose her will on ambitious male Protestants. As her life story makes clear, she showed intelligence, courage, determination, piety, compassion, dignity, generosity and no small amount of personal charm. On discovering the dilemmas she faced, and learning how she tackled them, it not difficult to sympathise.

Her enduring popularity can be attributed to various factors – the novelty of a female monarch (though her reign coincided with those of Mary I and Elizabeth I of England); the romantic sweep of her adventures; the youthful beauty that won her admirers in her own time; the tragic aspect of her ultimate undoing.

In the end, though, it cannot be denied that the personality emerging from the accounts of her life – even those written by her detractors with the express purpose of blackening her character – is one that is hard not to like.

1542

23 November

Lochmaben Castle Prelude

The winter of 1542–3 was going to be harsh: both bitterly cold and cruelly violent. At the medieval stronghold of Lochmaben, a few miles from the border with England, the King of Scotland was making preparations for war.

James V was troubled and unwell, but filled with purpose. The English people, just beyond the Solway Firth, were soon to bear the full brunt of his fury. He had come here to carry out an act of vengeance, a bold assertion of power, a ruthless signal that he was not to be trifled with.

His father had found himself in a similar position 29 years earlier. James IV had been a role model to aspire to: ambitious and courageous, cultured and pious, a true Renaissance prince. He had established himself as a prominent figure on the European stage.

He had even sealed a crucial Treaty of Perpetual Peace with England, the 'Auld Enemy', cementing it with an enviable diplomatic marriage – to Margaret Tudor, daughter of Henry VII of England. James IV's country might be small and poor, relative to its neighbour to the south, but it had a strong sense of its own identity, a cultured court and high aspirations.

But in 1513, the 'perpetual' peace was shattered. James IV had chosen to honour a much older alliance. When Louis XII of France was faced with an invasion by Henry VIII of England, he had appealed to James IV for help.

After weighing up his options, James had declared war on England. In September 1513, he had marched into Northumbria at the head of a vast army, somewhere between 20,000 and 35,000 men. It should have been a simple distraction, enough to divert Henry's attention to the north of England, relieving the pressure on France.

Instead, it had been an utter disaster. Engaging an English force at Flodden Field in Northumbria, James IV was killed, together with thousands of his followers. His son became James V at barely a year old.

Three decades later, a similar situation had arisen. When Margaret Tudor died in 1541, her brother Henry had revived English claims to overlordship of Scotland. He was also preparing for an invasion of France.

Anticipating an attack from the north, Henry pre-empted it in August 1542, sending a 3,000-strong army into Scotland. This was met and defeated at Haddon Rig, near Kelso, by a Scottish force led by the Earl of Huntly.

1 An etching of Loch Maben, with the castle at its centre.

2 Mary's father, King James V.

3 Lochmaben Castle today.

Henry was not slow to retaliate, ordering the Duke of Norfolk to assemble forces for a full-scale invasion. James sent commissioners to York in a vain bid to negotiate a truce. Meanwhile, he assembled an army at Edinburgh. On 22 October, Norfolk invaded southern Scotland, pillaging and burning as he came. But his army was poorly supplied and eventually withdrew south of the border. An English fleet sent to support it attacked at Eyemouth and later anchored in the Firth of Forth, but eventually withdrew.

James had by now led his army to Fala Muir, just north of the Borders. On learning of Norfolk's retreat, he hoped to press home his advantage, but his army was not prepared for an invasion of England and soon disbanded. James, humiliated and furious, swore that there would be a military strike against England 'before the light of this moon has ended'.

James then mustered two forces. The first was under Cardinal Beaton, the head of the Church, and James's half-brother the Earl of Moray. The other was commanded by himself and Lord Maxwell. It was a substantial army – perhaps over 15,000 men – but ill-disciplined and lacking a clear network of command.

The Protestant reformer John Knox described James's recruitment process as follows: 'To him comes companies from all quarters, as they were appointed, no man knowing of another (for no general proclamation passed, but privy letters), neither yet did the multitude know anything of the purpose ...'

James himself was distracted from the task in hand. First, there was his illness, in which stress was very likely a factor. In a letter to his French wife, Mary of Guise, probably from Lochmaben, James wrote: 'I have been very ill these three days past, as I never was in my life; but God be thanked I am well.' But James was not healthy enough to lead his men into battle.

And then there was the question of an heir. Little more than a year ago, the king could boast two legitimate sons. Then, on 21 April 1541, came an unthinkable catastrophe: both boys died on the same day, swept away by illness.

Now, though, Mary of Guise was in the advanced stages of pregnancy again, so there were grounds for hope. The birth was expected any day. The Stewart line of monarchs – of whom James was the seventh – hung in the balance.

Mary's Visit

Mary herself would visit the scene of her father's invasion plans some years later, and in happier circumstances. In early October 1565, two months after their marriage, she and her second husband, Lord Darnley, enjoyed a banquet at Lochmaben Castle. They had good reason to celebrate: Mary had seen off a rebellion by her half-brother James Stewart, Earl of Moray, leading her own army in a relentless pursuit known as the Chaseabout Raid (see page 68).

James's dames

Mary of Guise (*above*), the mother of Mary Queen of Scots, was James V's second French wife. The first was Madeleine of Valois, daughter of King Francis I. She married James aged 16, and came to live in Scotland in May 1537, bringing with her a handsome dowry. However, her health was frail and she died within two months.

Setting aside his paternal grief, Francis facilitated a second marriage. Mary of Guise was recently widowed, with one living son (her second son had died in infancy). She had caught James's eye when he visited France in 1536. Moreover, as a member of the powerful Guise family she was a good diplomatic match. With a view to blocking the marriage, Henry VIII of England wooed Mary, but she turned down his proposal, joking morbidly about her slender neck. (Henry was a notorious beheader of denounced wives.)

Mary was not particularly keen on James either – or at the prospect of moving to Scotland, which the French considered a backward and uncivilised country. But at the insistence of King Francis, she married James by proxy in May 1538. She too brought a substantial dowry, again boosting James's wealth and prestige. She spent most of the rest of her life in Scotland, and proved to be a shrewd politician, eventually governing the country as regent, some years after James's death.

Both Mary and Madeleine are represented among the carved oak roundels known as the Stirling Heads, commissioned by James around 1540 to decorate the palace ceilings at Stirling Castle.

Aside from his two wives, James took many mistresses and sired at least nine illegitimate children, probably all by different women. Although they were ineligible to be heirs to the throne, most of them were made nobles and some played significant roles in the life of their legitimate sister Queen Mary.

They included John Stewart, Prior of Fordingham, Mary's favourite sibling; Jean Stewart, also close to Mary; and James Stewart, an important ally in her early years, who later, as the Earl of Moray, played a key role in her downfall.

1542

A Time to be Born and a Time to Die

Mary Queen of Scots was not the first Stewart monarch to ascend the throne at a tender age; nor would she be the last. However, she was the youngest, becoming queen at just six days old.

The reign that began on 14 December 1542 would have been tumultuous for any sovereign. Both England and France were attempting to use Scotland as a pawn in their machinations against each other and other powers, including the Holy Roman Empire. Previous kings had been effective in asserting Scotland's independence, but it could not compete easily with the wealth and power of its near neighbours.

Meanwhile, Protestant ideas were sweeping through northern Europe, borne on a wave of church reform that inevitably licked at Scotland's Catholic shores.

Henry VIII of England had already broken with the Pope, and at home a charismatic young preacher named John Knox would soon gain a reputation as a zealous champion of the Reformation.

A succession of child monarchs meant that Scottish nobles had enjoyed much more opportunity to exercise their own authority – both in national affairs and in their own regions – than their counterparts in England. This was particularly true in the more inaccessible areas of Scotland, notably the west, which had only recently been brought under the control of the crown and even then only nominally. It also created the perfect conditions for family rivalries to flourish.

Scotland had fought hard for its independence and had a strong sense of its own identity. But for a newborn queen the political arena was, to say the least, something of a viper's nest.

▶ Linlithgow Palace, seen from across the frozen loch, with St Michael's Church to the left.

1542

8 December

Linlithgow Palace
Birth of a queen

We can pinpoint the spot where Mary gave birth to her son and successor, James VI (see page 76). The location of her own birth is not quite so precise, but we can hazard a good guess.

She was certainly born at Linlithgow Palace, a grand royal residence on the route between the two mighty castles at Stirling and Edinburgh. Despite its central location, this was something of a peaceful retreat for the Stewart monarchs, and several of Mary's ancestors had lovingly enlarged and embellished it.

While James V was at Lochmaben Castle, his wife Mary of Guise was preparing to give birth in her chambers at Linlithgow. She had a strong affinity with the palace, having declared it as fine as any French château. (As a Guise, she was familiar with some of the best, and there was probably an element of tact and diplomacy in this remark.)

Her apartment may have been in the north range. We cannot be sure because it collapsed in 1607, and was later replaced with the present structure.

Another possible location is the west range, built as a royal lodging by James IV around 1500–03.

His consort, Queen Margaret, may well have occupied the floor above his apartment – and perhaps also the tower at its corner, which is still known as Queen Margaret's Bower. In any case, as James V's wife, Mary probably used the accommodation formerly occupied by his mother – indeed, he himself had been born here, probably in the same chamber.

The winter of 1542–3 was particularly bitter, but the palace interiors would have been warm and colourful, with coal fires blazing in the grates and the stone walls insulated with rich tapestries and hangings, and perhaps gilded wooden panelling.

This was the fifth time Mary had given birth, so she knew what to expect. What she couldn't have expected was the mood of her husband. Vigorous and ambitious but vain and neurotic, he was overwhelmed by the defeat at Solway Moss (see page 14). He came to Linlithgow after the battle but soon departed for Edinburgh and then Falkland. He was desperate for an heir, but too shaken to await the child's arrival.

So the baby girl who first drew breath on the Feast of the Immaculate Conception of the Virgin Mary was born under something of a shadow.

Rumours soon spread that she had been born prematurely – 'a verye weyke childe and not like to lyve, as it is thought'. One letter to Henry VIII informed him that she had in fact perished. But her health soon rallied.

She was baptised in some haste at St Michael's Church, adjacent to the palace, and Mary of Guise wasted little time quashing any damaging tittle-tattle. At three months, she was presented naked to the English envoy, Sir Ralph Sadler, who reported her to be 'as goodly a child as I have seen of her age'. By then, of course, she was a queen.

1542 24 August	24 November	8 December	14 December
Battle of Haddon Rig: Henry VIII of England tries to force James V to abandon the Catholic Church. Scottish forces repel English.	**Battle of Solway Moss.** Scottish forces are routed following a raid on Cumbria.	**Mary is born** at Linlithgow Palace.	**James V dies** at Falkland Palace.

3

1 The later north range of Linlithgow Palace, with Queen Mary's Bower at the left.

2 Mary of Guise, mother of Mary Queen of Scots.

3 An illustration of the fountain at Linlithgow Palace as it may have looked when first completed.

Later Visits

Mary spent her first seven months at Linlithgow, where she and her mother the dowager queen would have been thoroughly cosseted by the ladies of the court. She may have found crawling a challenge on the bare stone slabs of the courtyard, but doubtless she enjoyed the sparkling water and bright colours of the fountain her father had installed there.

In July 1543, she was moved to the greater safety of Stirling Castle, where she lived for the next few years. She did not stay at Linlithgow again until September 1561.

She also visited the palace in early December 1566, hoping to recuperate from a pain in her right side. This was a recurring malady which plagued her throughout her life, but on this occasion it may have been related to her pregnancy: her son would be born a little over six months later.

Her final visit to Linlithgow was an overnight stay on 23 April 1567, the night before she was abducted by Bothwell (see page 92).

It was in Linlithgow that Mary's most troublesome sibling, James Stewart, Earl of Moray, met his death. Having been appointed regent, to govern Scotland until James VI came of age, he was shot by an assassin on 11 January 1570. On learning of this, Mary arranged a pension for the sniper.

How Scottish was Mary?

As the only surviving legitimate child of King James V, Mary had an unimpeachable claim to the Scottish throne. But her mother was French; her paternal grandmother was English; her great-grandmother was Danish; her great-great-grandmother came from Guelders and her great-great-great grandmother from England. So her gene pool was at most 1/32nd Scottish. And that's without taking into account the fact that the Stewarts were descended from Normans. (And many of the Normans were of Norse descent.)

If the Jacobite rebels of the 1700s had been successful in their efforts to restore the Stuart monarchy, they would have placed on the throne Mary's great-grandson Prince James Francis Edward Stuart, a man whose blood was less than 1/250th Scottish, and who barely set foot in Scotland.

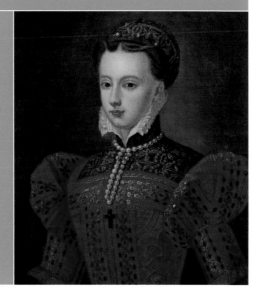

1542

14 December

Falkland Palace, Fife
It cam' wi' a lass;
it will gang wi' a lass

1

Like so many members of the Stewart dynasty, Mary was thrust to the throne at a very early age, as yet another promising young monarch fell dead in his prime.

Poor James. The vaulting ambition he had fostered and striven to achieve throughout his youth had crumbled and evaporated. Despite his illustrious travels, his wide and assiduous studies, his persuasive diplomacy with European potentates, his chivalric honours, his auspicious French marriages, his grand building schemes, all had come to naught.

At just 30, he was washed up. His nobles had abandoned him, leaving him to humiliation at Fala Muir and Solway Moss. His bonny male heirs had been swept away by illness, and now his own health was failing.

When the news arrived that his new baby heir was a girl and not the hoped-for boy, he fell into a terminal decline. His illness took hold again and he reportedly took to pronouncing doomy prophesies of his own death.

Most famously, he is recorded as saying, 'Adieu, farewell. It cam' wi' a lass; it will gang wi' a lass.' This is universally interpreted as a despairing account of the Stewart dynasty, which now seemed destined to die out. The lass it came with was Marjorie Bruce, daughter of King Robert I. It was her son, Robert II, who began the royal Stewart line.

As for the final lass, James was both right and wrong. The final Stewart monarch was female, but she was not his daughter.

⚔

25 November 1542
The Battle of
Solway Moss

John Knox, the notorious Protestant reformer, describes the preamble to this battle in typically vivid terms. 'After midnight ... the trumpet blew, and commanded all men to march forward, and to follow the King (who was constantly supposed to have been in the host). Guides were appointed to conduct them towards England, as both faithfully and closely they did. Upon point of day they approached to the enemy's ground; and so passed the water [the border] without any great resistance made unto them. The foray goes forth, fire rises, hership [ravaging] might have been seen on every side. The unprovided people were altogether amazed; for bright day appearing, they saw an army of ten thousand men; their corns and houses upon every side send flames of fire unto the heaven.'

Having begun to rain vengeance on the unfortunate residents of Cumbria, however, the Scottish army found itself confronting an English force led by Sir Thomas Wharton. The scene was Solway Moss, a boggy region on the edge of the River Esk.

At around this point, word spread among the Scots that the king was not present, and that they were under the command of an elderly retainer, a favourite of James named Oliver Sinclair.

Many of those present considered Robert, 5th Lord Maxwell the king's proper deputy – he had taken the lead in assembling the army.

The English troops were far fewer in number, but under Wharton's confident leadership they were well organised and highly motivated. The confusion over the chain of command had weakened the Scots' resolve. Many of them dropped their weapons and fled, rather than face the wrath of a disciplined English force.

Casualty estimates vary, but a grand total of 27 people are thought to have died during this battle. However, well over a thousand Scots were captured, among them Maxwell. Worse still, several hundred were said to have drowned while trying to escape.

For James, this was utter humiliation. When the news was brought to him at Lochmaben, he broke down. 'Oh, fled Oliver? Is Oliver ta'en?' he is recorded as saying, over and over again, as he fretted, sleepless, through the cold night.

The dynasty was to continue for more than 170 years, ending with the death of Queen Anne, the 15th Stewart sovereign, in 1714.

Whether from choice or ill health, James never saw his daughter. He visited Mary of Guise briefly at Linlithgow before she gave birth, then perhaps returned to Holyrood before departing for Fife. He visited Hallyards, the home of his treasurer, Sir William Kirkcaldy of Grange, whose wife attempted in vain to comfort him, and then departed for Falkland Palace.

Set in the forests of Fife and largely used as a grand hunting lodge, Falkland was a favourite royal residence. The old castle had been transformed into a sophisticated Renaissance palace by James IV, and James V had himself embellished it considerably. His additions include the twin circular towers of the gatehouse – now the palace's most distinctive feature – and carved heads, similar to the Stirling Heads but carved in stone. It may have seemed a peaceful retreat for a man clearly in some despair.

The 16th-century chronicler Robert Lindsay of Pitscottie records that on 14 December, with his senior noblemen gathered around him, 'He turned him upon his Back, and looked, and beheld all his Nobles and Lords about him, and gave a little Smile of Laughter, then kissed his Hand, and offered the same to all his Nobles round about him; thereafter held up his Hands to God, and yielded his Sprit to God.'

Mary's Visits

Mary was a keen huntswoman – one of her favourite fancy dress outfits was that of Diana, goddess of hunting. She certainly came to Falkland to enjoy both hunting and hawking. Deer were brought here specifically to be released for the hunt, though they were not always killed. Her first adult visit was in late September 1561, the month after her return to Scotland, and she was to return numerous times.

She also practised archery and played tennis here – the 'real' tennis court, or cachespule, was built for James V in 1539 and still survives, one of the oldest in Britain. The palace is only 13 miles from Wemyss Castle, where she would encounter her cousin, Lord Darnley, in February 1565.

The hereditary keepers of Falkland Palace belonged to the Beaton family and included the father and grandfather of Mary Beaton, one the queen's 'Four Maries'.

1542-8

The Little Queen

Mary's early childhood was overshadowed by one key question: who was she going to marry? Even as she lay gurgling in her crib, blissfully oblivious to her fate, matchmaking negotiations were busily underway. Today, it seems bizarre and even distasteful to be contemplating marriage for an infant, but it was a question with huge political implications, and quite normal in this era.

All monarchs were expected to produce heirs. If they did not, the dynasty from which they sprang would die out, leading to instability and the ascendancy of rivals. Perhaps just as important was the diplomatic alliance that could be sealed by a prestigious marriage. There might also be a valuable dowry to secure, as there had been for Mary's father. What did love have to do with it?

In the 1540s, Scotland had a crucial role to play in the balance of power between England and France. If Mary married into the royal family of either country it would gain a huge strategic advantage over the other. For centuries, Scotland had traditionally sided with France against England in an arrangement that came to be known as the Auld Alliance.

That was precisely what Henry VIII was determined to prevent. An old English adage said, 'Who that intendeth France to win, with Scotland let him begin.' Henry foresaw a united Britain, with himself as its ruler, bringing France to its knees. He had a five-year-old son, Prince Edward, who was heir to the throne and surely a perfect match for Mary.

For their part, the French had no husband to offer – not yet. But the influence of Mary's shrewd and dynamic French mother, Mary of Guise, combined with the strategic distribution of French pensions (essentially bribes) to Scottish nobles kept the pro-France faction in business.

Henry began with a charm offensive, releasing Scottish hostages and sending friendly emissaries to Scotland, but when this failed he played the bully and ultimately resorted to war.

▶ Stirling Castle, where Mary spent most of her early childhood.

1543

9 September

Stirling Castle
The head that wears the crown

At less than a week old, Mary became queen, the sixth in a string of seven child monarchs. By the time of her coronation, her ambitious nobles were already jostling for power and influence.

Mary was to spend most of her early childhood at Stirling Castle. This was a heavily armed fortress, amply defended both by its position on a crag and by military fortification. A royal castle since the early 1100s, its splendour had been greatly enhanced by Mary's grandfather, James IV. He commissioned the vast great hall, and the imposing forework with its four-towered gatehouse (now reduced in height and masked by 18th-century defences).

But its brand-new centrepiece was the royal palace, built, furnished and decorated to the specifications of Mary's parents, James V and Mary of Guise. It is doubtful that James saw it completed, but his ambitions for it are very much in evidence. The fashions of 16th-century Europe and the aspirations of a Renaissance prince are writ large in its structure and decorative scheme.

1 An artist's impression of Mary's coronation, with Cardinal Beaton officiating.

The Honours of Scotland
2 Crown, **3** Sword and **4** Sceptre – first used together at Mary's coronation.

1543 11 February	1 July	July	9 September	11 December
Henry VIII of England forms alliance with Charles V, Holy Roman Emperor, against France.	**Treaty of Greenwich signed** between Scotland and England. It agrees to the future marriage of Prince Edward and Mary Queen of Scots, uniting the two kingdoms.	The **Third Act of Succession** restores Mary Tudor and Elizabeth to the line of succession for the English Crown.	**Mary crowned** at Stirling Castle.	**Scotland rejects** the Treaty of Greenwich.

The exterior had countless carvings, including statues of Classical gods, saints, ancient kings, men-at-arms, *putti* (cherubs) and James V himself. These were probably painted in bright colours. The interior was certainly sumptuously painted in the grotesque style (inspired by decorations in the recently rediscovered grottoes of ancient Rome). The walls were hung with priceless tapestries and other rich hangings. At least one ceiling was embellished with large oak roundels carved to represent human figures – the famous Stirling Heads.

The palace's royal apartments included six grand chambers – three each for the king and queen. This arrangement survives, and the decorative scheme has been re-created by Historic Scotland, drawing on years of expert research and working with highly skilled craftspeople.

As monarch, Mary was theoretically entitled to occupy the king's chambers. As a small child, it is more likely that she was kept warm and comfortable in more modest surroundings – perhaps in the king's old building, a residential block built for James IV.

5 A statue of Saturn, one of the Classical figures adorning the royal palace at Stirling Castle.

The grandest occasion at Stirling during Mary's early years was her coronation, held in the chapel royal. (This building no longer stands; it was replaced in 1594 by the present chapel royal.) This was a state occasion of the highest solemnity, not least because it was the 30th anniversary of the disastrous Battle of Flodden. Sir Ralph Sadler reported sniffily to the English court that the festivities were 'not very costlie' – and by English standards this was true.

The ceremony was conducted by Cardinal David Beaton, Archbishop of St Andrews and head of the Church in Scotland. Also officiating were the country's most senior noblemen. James Hamilton, 2nd Earl of Arran – now governing the country as regent – bore the crown. Matthew Stewart, 4th Earl of Lennox held the sceptre and Archibald Campbell, 4th Earl of Argyll the sword. This was the first time the Honours of Scotland – our crown jewels – had been used together.

This was not a harmonious gathering. Beaton and Arran had already been at work attempting to discredit one another, and although Arran was next in line to the throne, Lennox could also claim direct descent from James III. An infant monarch created a power vacuum that men in their position were poised to fill.

For her part, Mary howled lustily throughout the ceremony.

Later Visits
Stirling was one of the nation's principal royal seats and Mary returned many times. See pages 82–3 and 90.

1544 19 January	11 April	May	3 May	19 July–18 September	18 September
Birth of Francis, dauphin of France, Mary's future husband.	**Battle of Ceresole:** French forces defeat those of the Holy Roman Empire.	**Charles V, Holy Roman Emperor,** invades eastern France.	**Edward Seymour, Earl of Hertford,** leads an English army to capture Edinburgh.	**Siege of Boulogne:** Henry VIII's forces take the town, but cannot push further into France.	**Peace of Crépy:** Peace is declared between the Holy Roman Empire and France. War continues between France and England.

Fear and loathing in St Andrews

As the Catholic mother of a child queen in a country where Protestant ideas were taking hold, Mary of Guise found a natural ally in Cardinal David Beaton, Archbishop of St Andrews. Beaton was the most powerful churchman of his day, only the third Scot ever to attain the status of cardinal, and the first since 1387.

He was shrewd and well educated, and he had good connections in Europe, having studied in Paris and carried out a number of diplomatic missions. At the time of the Rough Wooing, he was the loudest voice opposing the pro-English, Protestant faction led by Regent Arran.

But for all his devotion to the Catholic faith, he was not a man of great piety or virtue. Rumours spread by his enemies suggested an affair with Mary of Guise. This is highly unlikely, but he certainly flouted his vows of chastity, openly consorting with at least one mistress, Marion Ogilvy, who bore him no fewer than eight children. (This was not unusual among churchmen of the period, however.)

Soon after James V's death, Beaton produced a will, almost certainly forged, which he claimed appointed him as head of the council and governor of the young queen. After becoming regent, Arran saw the need to neutralise Beaton, and initially attempted appeasement.

In January 1543, he made Beaton chancellor, but this was a short-lived plateau in their hostile relations. Arran was famously indecisive, and must quickly have found it an unsatisfactory solution. A fortnight later, he contrived to have Beaton imprisoned.

The cardinal was held at Blackness Castle on the Firth of Forth, but by the summer he was free: the rumour was that little attempt had been made to keep him guarded. According to the chronicler Robert Lindsay of Pitscottie, he immediately 'began to rage as any lion loosed of his bond'. By September, he had forced Arran to agree to share power and headed off an attempt to take Mary to England, which led Henry VIII to call for his assassination.

In the end, though, Beaton was the victim of Scottish wrath. On 1 March 1546, he had the Protestant preacher George Wishart burned at the stake for heresy — attaching bags of gunpowder to the unfortunate man for a spectacular finish.

Wishart was a firebrand and a heretic, but had the reputation of being a gentle soul, and even zealous Catholics were appalled. This atrocity helped galvanise Beaton's enemies into action. A few weeks later, at around 6am on 29 May, a party led by Fife lairds gained access to St Andrews Castle, Beaton's official residence, by posing as stonemasons. They made their way up the stairs to his private chambers where he, sensing trouble, bolted the door. The intruders heaped burning coals outside it and eventually broke in. Beaton was harangued as a 'vile papist' and then stabbed repeatedly.

Shortly afterwards, the cardinal's mutilated body was to be seen hanging naked from the walls of his castle. To compound the sacrilege, one of the assassins urinated from the ramparts into the corpse's mouth.

These lurid events marked the beginning of a siege that was to last more than a year. The Protestant lairds, who came to be known as 'Castilians', barricaded themselves inside the castle, taking hostages. One of these was Arran's son, whom he aspired to marry to Mary: this delicate situation was one factor in prolonging the siege. Beaton's body, meanwhile, was preserved in salt and kept in the notorious bottle dungeon, a subterranean prison cell.

Arran's engineers began to tunnel towards the castle's foundations, aiming to undermine its defences. For their part, the Castilians began digging a countermine, and eventually intercepted the siege tunnel. At some point, their number was swelled by the preacher John Knox, who had once acted as Wishart's bodyguard, fending off any would-be assailants with a two-handed sword.

The siege was finally brought to an end in July 1547 by an Italian seaman, Leone Strozzi. He commanded a French flotilla sent by Henry II, which moored in St Andrews Bay and bombarded the castle both from the sea and from neighbouring buildings, including St Salvator's College. The Castilians were swiftly forced to capitulate and the survivors were taken prisoner. Knox, among others, spent the next 18 months in forced labour on the French galleys.

1 Cardinal David Beaton.

2 St Andrews Castle, scene of Beaton's murder and the siege that followed.

1545 27 February	8 July	18-19 July	7 December	1546 1 March
Battle of Ancrum Moor: Scottish forces defeat a much larger English army, leading to a respite in the 'Rough Wooing'.	**Birth of Don Carlos,** son of Philip II of Spain.	**Battle of the Solent** between English and French fleets. No outright victory, but on 19 July Henry VIII's flagship, the *Mary Rose* sinks.	**Birth of Henry Stewart, Lord Darnley,** cousin and future husband of Mary.	**George Wishart,** a Protestant religious reformer, is burnt at the stake in St Andrews.

20

10 September 1547

The Battle of Pinkie Cleugh

The Treaties of Greenwich, signed on 1 July 1543, had two key purposes. The first was to establish peace between Scotland and England. The second was to agree a future marriage between Mary and Prince Edward, the son and heir of Henry VIII.

By December, Scotland's 'Auld Alliance' with France had been restored. The Scottish parliament threw out the treaties, citing Henry's seizure of Scottish ships – and his failure to ratify them himself. Henry was furious and launched a series of military strikes on Scotland known as the Rough Wooing.

In May 1544, he sent Edward Seymour, Earl of Hertford, to 'overthrow Edinburgh Castle, sack Holyroodhouse and burn and subvert it and all the rest, putting man, woman and child to fire and sword'. Though he failed to take Edinburgh, Hertford inflicted pillage and death on a grand scale. Further attacks followed in 1545.

In May 1546, the siege of St Andrews began, and England supported the Protestant rebels occupying the castle. They were only ousted by French military intervention in July 1547.

By then, Henry VIII and Francis I of France had both died, rupturing the balance of power. Seymour, now Duke of Somerset, had been appointed to govern England as Protector. He led one final round of Rough Wooing, marching north with an army of at least 15,000.

The Scots, under Regent Arran, were well prepared, and an army of some 35,000 – the largest in Scottish history – was strategically positioned a few miles east of Edinburgh, blocking the route to the city between marshland and the coast.

There was every possibility that the Scots might repel the invading force, the terrain proving difficult for the English cavalry, but the traditional pike charge proved no match for Somerset's well-disciplined forces. The Scots were decimated by artillery fire from English ships moored in the Firth of Forth, and by experienced English cavalrymen.

Arran's courage then failed. Notoriously, he fled, and for many of his troops this was the signal to drop their weapons and flee. The bloody scene was vividly described by the Englishman William Patten: 'a pitiful sight of the dead corpses lying dispersed abroad, some their legs off, some but houghed [hamstrung], and left lying half-dead, some thrust quite through the body, others the arms cut off, diverse their necks half asunder, many their heads cloven, of sundry the brains pasht out, some others again their heads quite off, with other many kinds of killing.'

Some 10,000 Scotsmen were killed and 2,000 taken prisoner. It was a disaster on the scale of Flodden.

3 A contemporary illustration of the battle.

4 Edward Seymour, Earl of Hertford.

5 Regent Arran.

1546 29 May	7 June	1547 28 January	4 February	31 March	10 September
Protestant rebels break into St Andrew's Castle, assassinate Cardinal Beaton and occupy the castle.	**The Treaty of Ardres** secures peace between England and France, ending the Italian War that began in 1542.	**Henry VIII dies.** His nine-year-old son Edward VI succeeds him as king.	**Edward's uncle, the Earl of Hertford,** is made Duke of Somerset and Lord Protector of England, governing on Edward's behalf.	**Francis I of France dies.** His son Henry II succeeds him as king.	**Battle of Pinkie Cleugh:** Somerset's army defeats the Scots forces. He establishes a network of forts in southern Scotland.

1547

11 September

Inchmahome Priory, Lake of Menteith
An island retreat

1 A 19th-century map of the Lake of Menteith, showing Inchmahome and neighbouring Inch Talla.

2 The boxwood trees of Queen Mary's Bower.

3 The priory's cloister.

4 One of island's gnarled sweet chestnut trees.

After the disaster of Pinkie, Scotland's main power centres, Edinburgh and Stirling, suddenly lay vulnerable to English attack. Even the mighty fortress of Stirling Castle seemed an unsafe place to keep the young queen. So, under cover of darkness, she and Mary of Guise were quietly carried by litter and boat to a tiny inland island, idyllic home to an Augustinian priory.

Inchmahome Priory had been founded in 1238 by the Comyns, at that time one of Scotland's most powerful families. They reached the peak of their powers at the start of the 1300s, but were ruthlessly wiped out by Robert the Bruce after he seized the throne in 1306. One of their chief seats was Inch Talla, a tiny island next to Inchmahome.

The Lake of Mentieth lies 15 miles west of Stirling, and is the only body of water in Scotland officially known as a lake. It is still a beautiful and calm setting, and must have seemed remarkably peaceful compared to bustling Stirling.

The Augustinian canons would have continued their daily round of prayer and manual labour while Mary was their guest, but they must have felt a certain degree of tension. It was not at all unusual for abbeys and priories to bear the brunt of English invasion, not least because they generally held a good deal of portable wealth. Fortunately, the priory bore its weighty responsibility without incident. The prior, it seems, was even able to teach his charge some Latin.

The guest chambers in monasteries were usually located in the west range of the cloister, but unfortunately nothing survives of these buildings at Inchmahome. However, it is easy to imagine the young Mary, then aged almost five, exploring the forested paths of the island. Three sweet chestnut trees, now twisted and gnarled, are said to date back to Mary's day.

Mary only stayed on the island for three weeks, but it is testament to her legendary status that various features still bear her name. A lawn to the south-west of the priory is known as her garden, and a little bower of boxwood is said to have been planted by her – though it had to be replanted in 1859. In a book of 1880, Sir William Fraser noted that, 'The desire of tourists to become possessed of relics of Queen Mary has gradually led to the complete disappearance of nearly the whole of these trees.'

1548

29 July
Dumbarton Castle, West Dunbartonshire
All aboard for Saint-Pol-de-Léon

The Battle of Pinkie had been a triumph for the Duke of Somerset, who swiftly established forts in the south and east of Scotland. But its final outcome was not at all what the English expected or wanted.

The Rough Wooing had essentially been an attempt to bully the Scots into surrendering their child queen for marriage into English royalty, allowing England to claim sovereignty over its neighbour. Instead, it drove the Scots into dynastic union with the French.

Arran, who rarely acted so decisively, quickly agreed terms with Henry II of France (and was made Duke of Châtelherault by the French king as a reward). Mary was pledged to Henry's son Francis, the dauphin, or heir to the throne.

With the English garrison besieged by French forces at Haddington, parliament approved a crucial marriage that would unite the Scottish and French crowns.

Since February 1548, Mary had been living at Dumbarton Castle. Standing on a tall rock, at the point where the Firth of Clyde narrows to a river, this was the ancient royal stronghold of the Brythonic kingdom of Strathclyde. It had been successfully besieged by the Vikings, but subsequently proved impregnable.

During these few months, Mary had suffered one of her many bouts of illness. At the time it was said to be smallpox, but it was more likely measles. Fortunately, she had fully recovered by the summer.

The French king sent his own royal galley to collect her, together with three other vessels. She boarded on 29 July with an entourage that included at least two of her half-brothers, and possibly Lord James, her eldest brother, later Earl of Moray. Also on board were the 'four Maries' – Mary Livingston, Mary Fleming, Mary Beaton and Mary Seton – noblewomen of about her age who would be her constant companions for some years, and in one case for the rest of her life.

Their departure was delayed for more than a week while they awaited a favourable wind. Suffering from ennui, the spirited Mary Fleming demanded to disembark, but was refused permission by the captain. On 7 August, the west wind picked up and the ships set sail for northern France.

5 Dumbarton Castle in an illustration of the 1690s.

Sad stories of the death of kings

Henry VIII of England (*right*) and Francis I of France (*left*) died within nine weeks of each other, on (respectively) 28 January and 31 March 1547. The deaths of these two powerful and enduring rivals dramatically altered the political complexion of northern Europe.

Francis was succeeded by his son, Henry II, who took a keen interest in protecting Scotland. In England, Edward VI became king aged nine. Henry's brother-in-law Edward Seymour, Earl of Hertford assumed control on his behalf, taking the title Duke of Somerset. He immediately resumed the Wars of the Rough Wooing, hoping to capture Edinburgh and establish a permanent English garrison in Scotland.

Until the Reformation Parliament of August 1560, Scotland was a Catholic country, under the religious authority of the Pope. After that date, the kingdom was officially Protestant, though it would take over a century before Presbyterianism was fully established as the accepted form of Protestant worship.

Attempts had been made to reform the Catholic Church in the years leading up to the Reformation. Measures included efforts to improve theological training to raise standards of preaching, limiting the clergy's secular duties –which took them away from spiritual work – and attempts to deal with the moral laxity of the clergy. In 1552, a catechism – or manual of doctrine – was printed in Scots language to ease teaching.

However, a significant problem was the financial structure of the church and no effort was made to address this. Parish revenues were commonly appropriated to cathedrals and religious houses, leading priests to take on several parishes in order to make a living. The result was that many parishes found themselves without a resident priest for much of the year. Also, the Protestant Reformers benefited from the political situation in Scotland around 1560, gaining support from those who feared increased French influence in politics.

Support was by no means universal though, and one of the biggest challenges facing Mary on her return to Scotland was the tension between the Reformers and those who, like the queen, still embraced the Catholic faith.

1

FAITH AND WORSHIP

Mary chose not to attempt a counter-reformation, despite offers of political and military support to do so. Instead, she accepted the status quo, provided she was allowed to continue to practise her faith herself. Mary was indeed permitted to hear Mass in private, most famously at Holyrood, but also while on progress around the country. This provoked opposition from many reformers, though Mary took steps to ensure that hearing Mass was a privilege reserved for her. Despite this, many feared that she would ultimately lead Scotland back to the Catholic faith.

When she was deposed in 1567, the General Assembly of the Kirk sought to gain ratification of the 1560 legislation, and to improve provision of trained clergy for the parishes. This second Reformation introduced no real changes in aim, but it was an indication that the new faith had failed to progress during Mary's reign.

Both forms of faith are of course branches of Christianity, but there were marked differences between them. In Catholicism, Mass was generally celebrated in Latin and thus the words were unintelligible to most worshippers. Bibles and other religious texts were usually in Latin as well. Mary owned several, even carrying a prayer book to her execution. Images in the form of paintings and statues were used to convey Bible messages.

Under the new faith, the use of vernacular language was required, so that the congregation could understand and participate in the service. Personal reading of the Bible was also to be a new part of religious practice and iconography was to be entirely removed. Saints' cults, holy and feast days and altars were banned after 1560, though Mary was permitted the use of a small oratory during her captivity at Lochleven Castle – it can still be seen today. The new faith encouraged a more direct relationship with God, so anything seen as interfering with that was to be abolished.

This was reflected in the structure of the new church. Presbyterian Protestantism – which abolished the hierarchy of archbishops and bishops – was not the official form until 1690, but even in 1560 many reformers favoured it. It was the monarchy which preferred an Anglican-style hierarchy, retaining Crown-appointed bishops who could be used to control the church and thus its revenue. This tension contributed to the outbreak of civil war in the British Isles in the 1640s, ultimately leading to the overthrow and execution of Mary's grandson Charles I.

The Reformation also had a significant impact on Scottish culture. Prior to 1560, the Church was a key patron of artists and musicians, employing them to decorate church buildings and compose liturgical music.

With the abolition of iconography and the focus on Psalms rather than hymns, this patronage was discontinued.

Scotland also began to forge stronger links with other Protestant countries such as England, at the expense of its traditional relationship with Catholic France, and this would influence cultural developments. Changes in how the new faith was practised would also come to have an impact. For instance, confession was no longer a private matter between priest and sinner. Instead, both confession and penance were public and were carried out before the entire congregation.

These developments were slow to take shape, but their effects were felt in every sphere of life, throughout Scotland and the whole of Europe. They were undoubtedly a key destabilising factor in Mary's reign and life.

1 A French crucifix and rosary thought to have belonged to Mary.

2 A Puritan bible, dating from about 1560.

1548–61

La Petite Royne

Mary was brought to France partly to forestall any English attempt to kidnap her, but mainly to be groomed as a future queen. She was treated accordingly. France was a much wealthier country than Scotland, and Mary soon learned to enjoy luxury.

The party landed in Brittany on 13 August 1548, after a rough crossing. Most of the Scots had been seasick; indeed one young gentleman had died. But Mary – for once – had remained healthy. From the coast, they enjoyed a leisurely journey, mainly by barge, to the magnificent palace of Saint-Germain-en-Laye.

France was impressed. Antoinette, Duchess of Lorraine, matriarch of the Guise family, accompanied Mary for most her journey. Her letters of the time extol the beauty and intelligence of her granddaughter. Peasants shouted out, *'Vive la reinette!'* ('Long live the little queen') as the royal barge cruised past. The duchess's high opinion was soon seconded by King Henry II, Mary's future father-in-law.

Mary was to be thoroughly pampered, sumptuously dressed, exquisitely fed, lavishly entertained and brilliantly educated – her tutors would include Pierre Ronsard, known to his peers as the 'prince of poets'. And in due course, she would marry the heir to the throne – and become queen of France.

But these years were not always happy. Mary was parted from her protective mother, Mary of Guise, who stayed on in Scotland. Friction between the Catholic Church and the new Protestant ideas had already led to violent confrontation, mirroring similar strife in Scotland.

In France, Mary would suffer another of the serious illnesses that blighted her life. And she would ultimately lose her first husband.

▶ The Cathedral of Nôtre-Dame, Paris, where Mary married the dauphin of France.

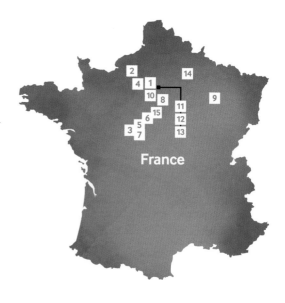

France

1 Château de Saint-Germain-en-Laye
2 Rouen
3 Château d'Amboise
4 Château d'Anet
5 Château de Blois
6 Château de Chambord
7 Château de Chenonceau
8 Château de Fontainebleau
9 Château du Grand Jardin
10 Château de Meudon
11 Louvre Palais
12 Nôtre-Dame Cathedral
13 Hôtel de Tournelles
14 Rheims Cathedral
15 Hôtel Groslot

1548

16 October
Saint-Germain-en-Laye, Yvelines
A right royal welcome

The French court where Mary would spend the next 12 years was familiar to her mother, who had doubtless prepared her. She seems to have coped well with this sudden transition. The presence of her own companions, and the high status accorded to her by the king, must have helped. But it was also fortunate that she bonded quickly with the little boy who was to be her husband.

Saint-Germain had been the site of a royal palace since the 1120s. The château had been rebuilt by Francis I in the late 1530s and was among his favourite residences. Henry II would later add an expansive new royal complex, the *château neuf*.

At the time of Mary's arrival, however, the château was undergoing thorough cleaning, and the royal nursery was in temporary accommodation nearby at the medieval stronghold of Carrières. It was here that she first met the dauphin, Francis, then aged four, and his little sisters Elisabeth and Claude.

Henry II's personal life was complicated. In 1533, he had married Catherine de' Medici, a daughter of the powerful Florentine banking family known for their fabulous wealth.

It was a diplomatic wedding, arranged by the couple's fathers, and reportedly consummated under the supervision of Francis I, who noted, unpleasantly, that both parties had 'shown valour in the joust'.

Both were only 14, and the experience seems to have had a very detrimental effect on Catherine. She did not reach full puberty until the age of 21, and was long rumoured to be sterile. Countless remedies were administered before she finally fell pregnant, giving birth to the dauphin in 1544. After that she bore Henry nine further children, of whom six survived. However, none were very healthy, no doubt partly thanks to the various treatments she had undergone.

Soon after their wedding, Henry had begun a lifelong affair with a glamorous widow, Diane de Poitiers, 20 years his senior. Though he respected Catherine's status as consort, it was to Diane that he turned for personal and political support. Both women played important roles in raising the royal children.

Mary was a tall, spirited five-year-old; Francis a sickly and stunted four-year old. Yet despite their obvious differences, and the overwhelming pressure placed on them by their circumstances, they seem to have hit it off remarkably well.

The Scots were considered an uncouth race, and Henry wanted to ensure that Mary was properly trained for her leading role in the French court. He therefore decreed that she would live and be educated with his own children. She quickly became close to the royal siblings, and at Saint-Germain she shared a bedroom with Elisabeth.

	1548 7 July	29 July	30 July
	Mary is betrothed to the dauphin, heir to the French throne.	**Mary boards a ship at Dumbarton**, bound for France.	**The siege of St Andrews** is finally broken by a French fleet moored in the bay. Among the Castilians led in chains to work on French galleys is a young Protestant preacher, John Knox.

1550

1 Henry II.
2 Catherine de' Medici.
3 The expansive palace
   and gardens of
   Saint-Germain-en-Laye.

1 October
City of Rouen, Normandy
Making an entrance

Mother's pride

Mary of Guise's visit to France was heartily welcomed by Mary Queen of Scots, and the powerful bond of love between mother and daughter was renewed. But her stay was not without its tribulations.

She disembarked at Dieppe on 25 September and remained in France for a year. It soon became apparent that she was short of money, and in March the English ambassador to France reported that the court had grown weary of sponsoring her. The atmosphere was also soured at this time when Mary's governess Lady Fleming, mother of Mary Fleming, fell pregnant. It soon came out that she had been having an affair with Henry II.

Then, during the final weeks of her stay, her son Francis was stricken by a mystery illness and died in her arms, aged 15. He had been the eldest of her four sons, and the only one to survive infancy. The grieving mother who departed in September 1551 did not know it, but she was also parting from her daughter for the last time.

Mary had been living in France for almost two years when her beloved mother came to visit. For her it was a joyous occasion in itself, but there were two other purposes for Mary of Guise's journey. The first was her father's death; the second was a great celebration of the Auld Alliance – France's military union with Scotland against England.

The death of Claude, Duke of Guise in April 1550 brought great sadness to his daughter. She was unable to attend his funeral, but decided to visit France anyway, to the delight of her daughter Mary. This was the first time she had spent with her mother since leaving Scotland. It would also prove to be the last.

The solemnity surrounding the duke's death was soon lifted by a mood of festivity. Henry had decided to mount a major event to celebrate the ousting of English forces from Scotland and from Boulogne. He also wanted to trumpet the dynastic promise of his son's forthcoming betrothal to Mary. His ceremonial entry into the city was to be a grand pageant, a conspicuous display of French royal wealth and power, witnessed by his court and extended family.

The king and his son the dauphin were the centre of attention, but he had cast Mary and her mother in important supporting roles – they were to view the proceedings from a prominent platform draped in French royal blue with gold fleurs de lys.

The event was modelled on the triumphal parades of imperial Rome. Gloriously clad in white velvet and cloth of silver, Henry rode into the city on a golden float drawn by 'unicorns' – white horses fitted with horns. The procession included banners showing the cities that had been liberated by French forces and six life-size papier mâché elephants. A huge artificial whale wallowed in the River Seine; and there was a theatrical spectacular, in which 50 naked 'Brazilian savages' engaged in tribal warfare. The climax was a naval battle in which a ship actually exploded, killing some of the sailors.

Today, Rouen is a sprawling modern city with a charming medieval heart centred on the vast cathedral. The historical event most prominently memorialised is the execution of Joan of Arc in 1431. But the city can rarely have seen a more exciting or overblown spectacle than this.

4 The grand entry of
   Henry II into Rouen.

Henry II accorded his daughter-in-law-to-be high status in the royal family, second only to his son the dauphin. Mary embraced her new status without hesitation, and retained throughout her life a sense of entitlement to a very high standard of living.

Vast amounts of food and drink were consumed by the royal household and their retinue. The court accounts record that on 8 June 1553, the royal children and their staff enjoyed 23 dozen loaves of bread, 18 pieces of beef, eight sheep, four calves, 20 capons, 120 chickens or pigeons, three young goats, six goslings and four hares, prepared for them by a kitchen staff of 57.

The finest fabrics were purchased in quantity and garments made according to the latest European fashions (see pages 40-41).

Equally striking was the extravagant architecture of French royal châteaux, many of which survive today, though most have been elaborated or damaged in more recent centuries. Their ornate exteriors were matched by exquisite interior design and magnificent artworks: paintings, tapestries, frescos and statues. The surroundings were laid out as extensive formal gardens, and in many cases hunting parks lay close by.

Both Scottish and French courts were peripatetic: they moved from place to place, taking their belongings with them – including beds and other furniture, tapestries and carpets, and of course clothes. Enormous wagon trains were required to carry out each move: the retinue could be 18,000 strong.

1 Mary aged about 16, not long before her marriage to the dauphin.

PALATIAL SPLENDOUR

The châteaux where Mary spent time during her years in France include:

Amboise
On the River Loire, near Tours

Seated on a rocky spur, Amboise has an ancient history said to date back to Julius Caesar. It was much enlarged by Louis XI and Charles VIII in the 1400s, and Francis I spent much of his youth here, hosting extravagant balls and masquerades, and maintaining a menagerie that included lions and leopards. Leonardo da Vinci came to live nearby, at Francis's invitation. Henry II and his son, Francis II, both enhanced its defences.

At Amboise in April 1551, Mary was the intended victim of a murder plot involving a poisoned dish of frittered pears. The culprit, Robert Stuart, possibly one of the Castilians of St Andrews (see page 20), was eventually caught in Scotland and sent back to France to be hanged, drawn and quartered.

In March 1560 a Protestant plot to kidnap and overthrow Francis II led to an all-out attack on Amboise. This was ruthlessly avenged by the Guises, who tortured and executed 1,200 alleged conspirators.

Anet
Near the River Eure, north of Chartres

Built by Henry II for Diane de Poitiers, this sprawling palace features a statue by Jean Goujon of its owner as Diana, goddess of the hunt. Diane hosted soirées here for the literary figures of the time, and Mary is said to have recited to them from the poetry of her tutor Pierre de Ronsard. In a letter of 1550, the dauphin wrote that he had never slept better than in the king's bed at Anet. The château was used as a location for the James Bond film *Thunderball*.

Blois
On the River Loire, between Tours and Orléans

Francis I redeveloped one wing of this grand royal château, installing a magnificent Renaissance staircase in the courtyard and loggias (rows of open arches) overlooking gardens glittering with pools and fountains. Two bears were sent to Blois for the entertainment of the royal children, but they caused embarrassment by damaging the home of a neighbour, Dame Pillonne.

Chambord
On the River Loire, between Tours and Orléans

Commissioned by Francis I in 1518 and never completed, this magnificent French Renaissance château is the largest in the Loire valley, with more than 400 rooms and 365 highly ornate chimneys. It features four circular corner towers and four more around the main entrance. At its heart is an extraordinary double-spiral staircase. Francis I and Henry II used the château as a hunting lodge: Henry often prioritised hunting over state affairs.

Chenonceau
On the River Cher, near Tours

Built for Francis I in 1513, Chenonceau was given by Henry II to his mistress Diane de Poitiers, and became one of Mary's favourite châteaux. Diane is said to have taught her falconry here, and both took part in great royal hunts. The château stands on a set of piers on the river, and from her bedchamber Mary could view the water gushing beneath the building. Diane commissioned an extension in 1556, but the château was taken over by Catherine de' Medici after Henry's death.

Fontainebleau
Beside the Forest of Fontainebleau, 40 miles south-east of Paris

In the 1520s, Francis I began transforming this medieval stronghold into a Renaissance château, drawing inspiration from Classical ideas of order and simplicity. He and his son Henry II enhanced it immensely and filled it with superb works of art. When English ambassadors visited Mary here in 1555, they were forced to concede it was grander than Hampton Court Palace in London. In 1561, the poet Ronsard wrote tenderly of the widowed Mary walking at Fontainebleau, her mourning gown blowing around her like a sail.

Château du Grand Jardin, Joinville
In Haute-Marne, 120 miles east-south-east of Paris

Built in 1533—46 by Mary's grandfather Claude, Duke of Guise, this was a country retreat for the Guise family. Originally an annexe to the Guise stronghold at Joinville (destroyed during the 18th-century Revolution), it was designed for balls and festivities, and did not include bedrooms. Mary came here on various occasions, including during the year-long visit of her mother, Mary of Guise, in 1550—1, and after the death of her husband Francis II.

Meudon
On the south-western outskirts of Paris

The residence of Mary's uncle Charles, Cardinal of Lorraine, often visited by Mary, who wrote to her mother about its 'grotto', a two-storey chamber rusticated to resemble a cave. The cardinal and his uncle and predecessor were great patrons of the arts. François Rabelais is said to have written his great bawdy satires *Pantagruel* and *Gargantua* here in the 1530s.

2 The sprawling Château de Fontainebleau, originally a medieval fortress, transformed into a grand Renaissance palace by Francis I and Henry II.

3 Claude, Duke of Guise, Mary's grandfather. He was head of the Guise family until his death in 1550, and commissioned the Château du Grand Jardin at Joinville.

1558

19 April

Louvre Palace, Paris
Teenagers in love?

Today, the Louvre Palace is famous as a museum, home to one of the world's greatest art collections, with a striking modern glass pyramid at its centre. In Mary's day it was a grand royal residence, freshly upgraded by Francis I, and the first Renaissance building in the French capital.

It was Francis who had restored Paris to its medieval role as royal seat of power, though many of the key royal palaces were still in the Loire valley. It was in the great hall at the Louvre that Mary, now 15, was officially betrothed to the 14-year-old dauphin.

The ceremony was preceded by months of negotiation between Scottish commissioners, led by Mary's half-brother James Stewart (the future Earl of Moray). The key issue was Scottish sovereignty, which many Scots feared might be subsumed. The marriage contract finally agreed granted dual nationality to citizens of both countries.

The betrothal ceremony was conducted by Mary's uncle the Cardinal of Lorraine, and followed by a ball in the sumptuously decorated gallery of the palace.

Mary was by now on the brink of womanhood. She was tall and vivacious, and many contemporary witnesses commented on her beauty. The dauphin, by contrast, was stunted, awkward and sullen. It can hardly have been a perfect love-match, yet the couple seem to have held one another in genuine affection.

1 Mary and Francis depicted as king and queen of France.

2 Mary's uncle, Charles, Cardinal of Lorraine, who conducted the coronation ceremony.

A generous mistress

When in France, Mary was well known for her generosity towards her retinue, for whom she sought better conditions and higher pay. (She had learned this from her mother. When James V died in 1542, several of his household staff sought employment with Mary of Guise, who was known to pay better.) Partly as a result, Mary's household budget was overstretched, and problems arose paying bills and wages in the mid-1550s.

1558

24 September
Cathedral of Nôtre-Dame, Paris
The bride wore white

The wedding of Mary and Francis had been anticipated for more than a decade and had far-reaching dynastic implications. Henry II did not intend it to pass unnoticed.

The ceremony was held at the magnificent gothic cathedral of Nôtre-Dame. The host was Mary's uncle, Francis, Duke of Guise. Those in attendance included the extended royal and Guise families.

Mary's dress was white – in 16th-century France the royal colour of mourning. It was, by all accounts, a stunning creation, sparkling with diamonds. She wore her hair loose, another breach of convention, and surmounted with a gold crown studded with large jewels.

(During the wedding banquet it became too heavy to wear, and was held above her head by an attendant.)

Amid all the extravagant pageantry, Mary remained the centre of attention, casting a long shadow over her pallid bridegroom. He may not have looked like much of a catch, but she had written to her mother that morning, 'I account myself one of the happiest women in the world.'

The wedding ring was worn by the king himself until it was required during the ceremony. As the guests filed into the church, the crowds were showered with largesse in the form of gold and silver coins.

After the wedding Mass there was a private banquet, followed by a ball. Then the party progressed through the city, Francis on horseback and Mary in a golden float, returning for a huge state banquet, with dancing and other entertainments.

A flotilla of six artificial ships in gold, silver and crimson velvet made its way through the throng and was said to represent the voyage of Jason, the Greek hero. Jason, who captured the Golden Fleece, stood for Henry, who by marrying his son into Scottish royalty had laid the foundations of a Franco-British empire.

The festivities continued through the night and into the next day, moving to the Louvre Palace. The finale was a tournament at Tournelles, another royal palace in the city. Meanwhile, the newlyweds spent their first night at the Guise family's Paris residence, the Hôtel de Guise. They then departed to enjoy a peaceful honeymoon in Picardy.

The marital relations between Mary and Francis have attracted prurient speculation. It is clear that he was no dashing fairytale prince; indeed it is thought that his testicles had failed to descend. Their relationship may not have been sexual, but by all accounts it was close and warm. They failed to produce a child, which was of course a crucial function of royal marriages. It is unlikely that anyone laid the blame for this at Mary's door.

3 A royal procession at Nôtre-Dame Cathedral in 1722. The wedding of Mary and Francis would have been an equally grand affair.

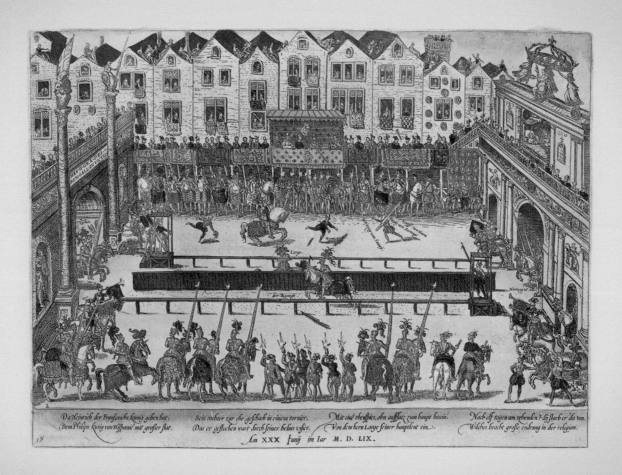

Da Heinrich der Frantzosischer kunig geben hat.
Dem Philips kunig von Hispania mit grosser stat.
Sein tochter zur ehe geschach in einem tornier.
Das er gestochen wart durch seines helms visier.
Mit einem rheussues, ohn aufflatz zum haupt hinein.
Von dem herrn Lorge seiner haubtlent ein.
Nach elf tagen am zehenden Julij starb er da von.
Welches bracht grosse entrang in der religion.

Am XXX Junij im Iar M. D. LIX.

1559

10 July

Hôtel de Tournelles, Paris
Le roi est mort – vive le roi

Henry II's great love of pageantry and jousting was, in the end, his undoing. His death aged 40 would propel the dauphin and his wife Mary to the French throne with unexpected haste.

The Treaty of Câteau-Cambresis, signed in northern France in April 1559, was an important landmark in the diplomatic relations of western Europe. It marked the end of the Italian wars, a struggle between Henry II and the Habsburg empire for control of Italy.

Peace treaties were often sealed with strategic weddings. In this case there were two. Philip II of Spain was to marry Henry's daughter, the Princess Elisabeth, Mary's childhood playmate. Meanwhile, Emmanuel Philibert, the warlike Duke of Savoy, was betrothed to Henry's sister, Margaret, Duchess of Berry.

But no celebration was complete without a tournament, as far as Henry was concerned. An event was duly held on 30 June at the Hôtel Tournelles, a 20-acre enclosure of parks, buildings and pleasure grounds close to the Bastille. Henry competed keenly, and at the end of the day demanded a rematch. His opponent was Gabriel, Count of Montgomery, a captain in the French Scots Guard, who had scored points against the king for a glancing blow in the previous round.

This time, Montgomery's aim was all too true. His lance hit the king squarely in the chest and shattered. Splinters shot up through the visor of the king's helmet and deep into his left eye. Every effort was made to save him, but he died 10 days later, surrounded by members of the royal household including Mary. (Catherine de' Medici made the most of her heightened status during her husband's incapacity. She exacted final vengeance on her husband and his long-term mistress, Diane de Poitiers, by refusing them access to each other.)

As Henry died, his son, Francis, was declared king. Mary stepped unhesitatingly into the role for which she had spent a decade preparing: she was now queen of France.

As for Montgomery: on his deathbed, Henry officially absolved the hapless captain of blame, but he found himself demonised and withdrew to his estates in Normandy, where he studied theology. He emerged a convert to Protestantism, and spent the rest of his life as a religious rebel. He was ultimately executed in 1574.

I could have told you that would happen

The famous mystic Michel de Nostradamus (*above*) is said to have predicted Henry's untimely death. He was a prominent figure at the French court in the 1550s and 60s, after Catherine de' Medici appointed him as her personal astrologer.

Henry's fatal accident is supposedly foretold in one of Nostradamus's notorious quatrains, which reads:

The young lion will defeat the old
On the field of combat in single duel
In golden armour, he will pierce his eyes,
Two wounds in one, then to die a cruel death.

The lions are of course said to be Henry and Montgomery, whose shields were reportedly decorated with lions. However, a contemporary illustration shows no lions – and no golden armour, come to that. Indeed, the supposed association between this verse and these events was not recorded until many years later.

It seems likely that the young Mary met Nostradamus at some point, but either he failed to foresee her ill-starred future or he kept it to himself.

▲ A 16th-century illustration of Henry II's fatal accident.

▼ Another contemporary illustration, showing Henry on his deathbed. Mary is shown in profile at the foot of the bed.

18 September

Rheims Cathedral
Nervous rex

The new king of France did not share his wife's gift for basking in the limelight. His coronation – at which Mary was relegated to the role of spectator – was a rather downbeat affair, despite lavish ceremonial trappings.

The event was held in the magnificent medieval cathedral of Nôtre-Dame at Rheims, in north-east France. Now inscribed as a UNESCO World Heritage Site, this soaring gothic marvel still retains stained glass dating back to the 1200s, despite being damaged by an English siege in 1359–60 and by German shells in 1914. This was a chief seat of the Church in France, and the traditional venue for coronations. The crown used had originally belonged to Charlemagne, the founding emperor of the Holy Roman Empire.

Uniquely among French kings, Francis II was crowned on a Monday. The service had been scheduled for Sunday, in keeping with tradition, but was postponed due to illness. The patient was Francis's new uncle by marriage, Emmanuel Philibert, Duke of Savoy: a battle-hardened warrior, he had been felled by a fever. A further inauspicious note was struck by gloomy weather and rainstorms.

Like the previous year's royal wedding, the ceremony was conducted by Mary's uncle, Charles, Cardinal of Lorraine and Archbishop of Rheims. The widowed queen mother, Catherine de' Medici, wore black, the colour of mourning in her native Italy, and her daughters followed suit.

True to form, Mary chose to stand out. She wore white, the French colour of mourning, which must have reminded observers of her unorthodox choice of wedding apparel.

The new king also began the ceremony dressed in white, but after being anointed with holy oil he changed into a splendid coronation gown in French royal blue decorated with golden fleurs-de-lys. Finally, after he had received the royal sceptre, rod and ring, Charlemagne's crown was lowered onto his head. It soon proved too heavy for him, and had to be held in place by a group of noblemen.

The ceremony lasted well over five hours, but it ended on an exhilarating note when hundreds of songbirds were released in the cathedral. History does not record how they were shooed out afterwards, or who cleaned up the mess.

Empire bulding

At the time of their coronation in France, Mary and Francis were announced as the king and queen of France, Scotland, England and Ireland. It became part of royal routine to style them in this way. A seal matrix – a mould for stamping sealing wax – was created for them, allowing them to seal documents as king and queen of all four countries.

This was all part of a campaign endorsed by Henry II and by the ambitious Guise family. It was witnessed by English ambassadors, who of course viewed it as shocking presumption. It would be used against Mary by her enemies in the English court for decades to come.

1 Mary's young husband, Francis, now king of France.
2 Rheims Cathedral.

1560

August
Château of Fontainebleau, Seine-et-Marne
Growing pains

A few months after she became queen of France, Mary suffered the most painful bereavement of her life. Mary of Guise, the adored mother she had been parted from for so long, died on 11 June 1560. She had been suffering from dropsy – swelling of the abdomen and legs caused by accumulation of fluid.

Mary of Guise had also suffered political defeat. By 1554, she had supplanted Arran to govern Scotland as regent. But in October 1559 she had been toppled by a cabal of Protestant nobles known as the Lords of the Congregation. They were led by the powerful Earl of Argyll and Mary's illegitimate half-brother, Lord James Stewart. And they had the support of England, where the Catholic Mary Tudor had been succeeded by her Protestant half-sister, Elizabeth I.

Mary of Guise was already very ill, but courageously assembled a French garrison and withdrew to the nearby port of Leith, which she fortified. French reinforcements were sent for but failed to arrive.

Hasty diplomacy between Philip II of Spain, Catherine de' Medici in France and Elizabeth in England led in July 1560 to the Treaty of Edinburgh. Under its terms, Mary and Francis would relinquish their claim to the English throne and recognise Elizabeth's right to rule, removing English emblems from their royal coat of arms. French troops would withdraw from Scotland. And in the absence of Queen Mary, Scotland would be governed by the rebel lords, paving the way for a Protestant Reformation.

Mary had followed these events closely, with mounting distress, but news of her mother's death was slow to reach her. The French authorities received word after a week, but kept it from her for a further 10 days, doubtless foreseeing her response. Mary, not yet 18, withdrew from public life for a month, and reportedly spent most of the time weeping. Her tutor, the poet Ronsard, movingly describes her floating through the gilded chambers and blooming gardens of Fontainebleau, adrift in a sea of grief.

However, Mary seems to have emerged from mourning a fully fledged adult, primed for the responsibilities of a queen of two nations. It was in August 1560 that she held her first one-to-one royal audience.

The meeting was with Sir Nicholas Throckmorton, an English Protestant representing Elizabeth I as ambassador to France. Throckmorton also knew Scotland – he had taken part in the Battle of Pinkie Cleugh (see page 21).

At this time, Throckmorton's unenviable task was to persuade Mary to ratify the Treaty of Edinburgh. In Mary's opinion, this would have been to betray herself, her dead mother and her religion. She seated Throckmorton on a low stool and skilfully outmanoeuvred him, reminding him that she and Elizabeth were cousins, sharing Tudor blood. She also requested the English queen's support, 'for I am sure she could ill bear the usage and disobedience of her subjects which she knows mine have shown unto me'.

Throckmorton was charmed and impressed. In a letter of 31 December 1560, he wrote: 'The Queen of Scotland doth carry herself so honourably, advisedly and discreetly, I can not but fear her progress. Methinks it were to be wished ... that the one of these two Queens of the isle of Britain were transformed into the shape of a man, to make so happy a marriage as thereby might be an unity of the whole isle.' He would later become a key player in Mary's life: despite their differences, an affectionate bond grew between them.

4 The English diplomat Sir Nicholas Throckmorton.

1560

5 December
Hôtel Groslot, Orléans
The final straw

1 Francis II , who died
   after barely a year as
   king.

▶ Robert Herdman's
   romantic painting
   'Mary Queen of Scots:
   The Farewell to France'
   (1867).

Francis II had always been a frail and pallid creature, and although he loved the trappings of royalty, he presented an unimpressive figure. There was also growing concern about his ability to sire a successor.

By the summer of 1560, Mary persuaded herself she was pregnant and began to dress accordingly. By the autumn, it became clear that no child was forthcoming. The Guise family downplayed this disappointment, stressing the youth of the royal couple and the many years of fertility that lay ahead.

But the signs were not promising.

Francis revelled in hunting, and was particularly keen on hawking. Like his father and grandfather, he had a reputation for indulging in these pursuits when he should be attending to affairs of state. It was on his return from hunting near Orléans in November that he collapsed from an illness originally diagnosed as an ear infection.

Francis was kept at the Hôtel Groslot, a Renaissance mansion built in the early 1550s by the local grandee Jacques Groslot. His condition worsened, and by the end of the month he was suffering discharges and seizures and had lost the ability to speak. Mary competed with her mother-in-law Catherine de' Medici to nurse the ailing king, but neither they nor the court physicians could effect a cure. On 5 December, his life petered out. He was not yet 17 and had been king for little over a year.

A few days shy of her 18th birthday, Mary was at a turning point in her life. In a few months, she had been doubly bereaved, losing two of her closest allies. She was no longer queen of France, and as dowager she enjoyed less power and fewer privileges. Meanwhile, her authority in Scotland had been violated. It was time to go home.

Mary set sail with a tearful string of 'Adieu's, predicting, quite correctly, that she would never see her beloved France again. Soon after embarking, she witnessed the sinking of a fishing boat, with all hands lost. Not surprisingly, she considered this a bad omen.

So it was under something of a cloud that she made her way home, accompanied by a retinue that included her four Maries, three Guise uncles and the diplomat Michel de Castelnau, who would stay on in Scotland as an ambassador.

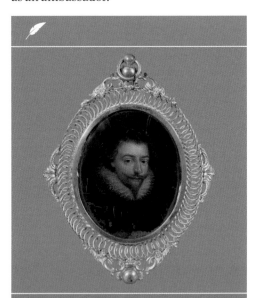

An admirable admiral

In 1560, a dashing young Scottish nobleman arrived in France. He was the Lord High Admiral of Scotland, sent with letters from Mary of Guise to her daughter, the young queen of France. On arrival, he was handsomely rewarded by the young king. This irked his many enemies at home, among them Regent Arran and Mary's half-brother Lord James, for he had a well-founded reputation as a hellraiser.

His name was James Hepburn, 4th Earl of Bothwell, and he was to play a major role in Mary's life.

▲ This miniature portrait, which hangs at the Usher Gallery in Lincoln, is said to depict James Hepburn, Earl of Bothwell, though its identification is unverified.

Clothing has always been used as a display of wealth, rank and power, and this was particularly true during the Renaissance. Anyone wearing extravagant clothing was readily identifiable as rich and powerful.

This was not just a matter of unspoken understanding. It was codified throughout Europe in 'Sumptuary Laws'. These were ostensibly designed to limit excessive spending on luxury items – but they were also intended to maintain the visual difference between people of different social classes.

In Scotland, the first of these laws was passed during the reign of James I (1406–37). It outlawed the wearing of fur for all but the highest classes. Similar laws followed in later years. We know that one was passed during Mary's reign, as on 5 January 1563 the English ambassador Thomas Randolph wrote of new Scotch laws 'about wines, great hose and costly apparel'.

However, it seems that they were not always obeyed. In 1581, James VI introduced a rather petulant sounding act. It declared that people of 'mean estate' were 'presuming to copy his highness and his nobility', and such people were not to wear 'any cloth of gold or silver, velvet, satin, damask, taffeta or any facing, fringing, trimming or embroidery of gold, silver or silk, nor yet linen, cambric or woollen cloth made and brought from any foreign countries'.

Court records from Mary's time show that a great deal of money was spent in acquiring these expensive fabrics for her own use.

Mary had over 50 gowns, and each would have been lavishly decorated with jewels and threads of gold and silver. Women's clothing could be combined in many different ways, so these 50 gowns could be styled in a wide variety of fashions.

Women generally wore a kirtle – initially a combined bodice and skirt which later became two separate items – over their under-layers. This would often be attached to separate sleeves, which would show from beneath a voluminous gown.

In the early 1500s, a ruff was formed at the neck by the chemise showing above the top of the gown. This gradually became more elaborate, and was cut higher, so as to be more visible. Blackwork, of black embroidery on white cloth, was a popular adornment of ruffs and other garments for both men and women.

Starch was introduced to Britain from Flanders in the 1560s, and this allowed the whole collar to be stiffened and shaped. This was achieved using heated rods called 'setting sticks', and large, flamboyant arrangements became possible. Eventually, this became a distinct garment, which could be washed separately – the ruff we now associate with Renaissance dress.

Another change during the century was in the farthingale – the series of hoops worn beneath the skirts to create a shape. During Mary's reign, this would have been a straight cone, from hip to floor.

FABRICS AND FINERY

1 Portrait of a nobleman dated 1569. The matching blackwork on the cuffs and ruff was popular in both men's and women's clothing. His doublet is shaped by 'bombast', a stuffing of flax, cotton or horsehair.

Later in the century, it became a wide hoop at the hips, falling in a straight line beneath. Gowns also tended to be closed at the front, without the colour of the kirtle showing beneath.

Fashions in dress for men were also changing. They wore five key pieces of clothing – a shirt, doublet, jerkin, hose and cloak. The doublet was a close-fitting garment worn over the shirt, and was often 'slashed', allowing parts of the shirt to be pulled through. The sleeves could be puffed out, or worn full and wide. They often had detachable, hanging sleeves, to add to the range of styles available.

The doublet might be lined with silk or taffeta, then stuffed with horsehair, flax or cotton. This padding was at first intended merely to give a smooth outline, and followed the contours of the body quite closely. Gradually, however, the fashion became more exaggerated and the doublet was padded to form a larger curve over the torso, stretching down into a point. This padding was known as 'bombast', which was the word for the soft down of the cotton plant. The hose would have been worn with a codpiece until the 1570s, and its shape was also accentuated by padding.

A jerkin was worn over the doublet – essentially this was a jacket. It took various forms, but after the 1540s it tended to be worn closed, with a low collar. Finally, the outer layer would usually be a gown or cloak, full and of rich fabric.

Clothing was adorned to emphasise the wearer's wealth – buttons and hooks were not merely functional, but items of jewellery in themselves, just as the fabric could include threads of precious metals.

Mary was well aware of the theatrical nature of dress. For masques and other courtly entertainments, she often commissioned themed clothing for herself and her courtiers. In 1564, for example, she hosted a masque at which all of the guests wore black and white.

However, Mary's whole life was a stage and her outfits were carefully planned to dazzle her audience.

At her first wedding in France, she insisted on wearing white, even though it was traditionally seen as the colour of mourning, and became known in France as 'The White Queen'.

Likewise, at her execution she wore a sombre black gown and white veil, giving an extraordinary air of dignity. When these were stripped from her, however, it was found that she wore a chemise of deep red – the Catholic colour of martyrdom. Mary's awareness of the theatricality of clothes, and the effect they could have on public opinion, was supreme.

2 Mary Beaton, one of Mary's close companions. Her cap, with the dip at the centre of the forehead, is of a style favoured by the queen herself, known as the Mary Queen of Scots Hood. She also wears a stiff, precise ruff, waist-chain, separate bodice and skirt and slightly padded sleeves beneath a flowing gown. The triangular farthingale is visible in the skirt's outline.

41

In Renaissance Scotland, jewellery was both functional and aesthetic. Today, restraint is considered an important element of good taste, but there were no such concerns to the nobility of the 1500s. They arrayed themselves in their finest jewels as conspicuous symbols of their wealth and status. Even as a child, Mary would have been bedecked in gold and silver, pearls and gemstones, the trappings of a crowned queen. Portraits of the period show extremes of adornment that reflect the way the nobility dressed in their everyday lives.

Mary's glittering jewellery collection was renowned. Inventories show that she brought 159 pieces to Scotland in 1561 and by the following year had acquired at least 20 more. Renaissance jewellery was usually made from yellow gold, lavishly decorated with soft enamels, diamonds, coloured gems and white pearls. Mary also had a famous string of 'black' or 'Tahitian' pearls, which are very rare. They were among her most prized possessions, and their colour was compared to Muscat grapes. On becoming regent in 1567, the Earl of Moray secretly sold them to Elizabeth I for £3,600. She is seen proudly wearing them in the 'Ermine portrait' of 1585.

Jewellery was not only a symbol of wealth; it was wealth. It had such value that it was ranked among a person's assets. It therefore played a very important social function in the giving of gifts. Mary had pieces of jewellery made as gifts for friends and supporters. A gift of jewellery was a powerful symbol of affection, loyalty and allegiance.

There are many accounts of such gifts. Some were given by Mary, whose generosity to her servants and subjects was well known; others were given to her by loyal supporters. Among the many surviving pieces is a stunning brooch, said to have been given by Mary to Mary Seton. Another is the famous Penicuik Necklace, thought to have been made up of bracelets given to one of her servants, Giles Mowbray, just before her execution.

Jewellery also served practical purposes. In the 1500s, people still believed in 'miasma theory'. Before the discovery of germs, it was thought that diseases were spread by bad smells, which might be caused by polluted water, poor hygiene conditions and other environmental factors, rather than being passed between people.

It was therefore thought that to wear a perfumed item of jewellery would offer some protection. Pomanders were hollow perfumed containers, often in the form of filigree beads, like those remaining in the Penicuik Necklace. They were made into chains and bracelets, or hung in single balls from neck-chains or belts. They would sometimes be made up of different sections, each containing a different perfume. Scents used included musk, ambergris and civet.

Rosary beads were of course essential to Catholics, each bead serving as memory aid for prayers to the Virgin Mary. They were often strung with a pendant in the form of a pomander. The wearing of crucifixes and rosaries was widespread amongst European Catholics in the 1500s. However in 1571, Elizabeth I banned the wearing of devotional jewellery, specifying them as 'ornaments called or named by the name of Agnus dei ['Lamb of God'], or any crosses, pyctures, beades or such lyke vayne and superstitious thynges from the Bishop or See of Rome'.

GEMS AND JEWELLERY

Mary herself habitually wore a gold cross, and owned several valuable rosaries. It seems she continued to wear these items long after the statute was passed. Indeed, we know that she carried a crucifix with her at the time of her execution.

Jewellery did not merely consist of individual pieces, but could adorn almost any part of costume. Gowns and doublets often had lavish buttons, items of jewellery in themselves, or were adorned with pearls and gems. Caps and hoods were trimmed with jewelled bands, or billiments, where precious stones alternated with pearl clusters. Mary and her courtiers would have demanded luxury goods imported from Europe and beyond, and the Edinburgh court would have been just as fashion-conscious as those of London and Paris.

However, very few pieces of jewellery from the period survive intact. This is partly because they were often melted down to obtain gold and silver for minting coins. The were also constantly re-set and refreshed in line with changing fashions and tastes. We know, for example, that Mary Seton's gifts were altered to create a larger set.

One piece that does survive from the period, and demonstrates the splendour of Renaissance jewellery, is the famous 'Lennox Jewel'. Made for Margaret Douglas, Countess of Lennox (Darnley's mother), it is a rich celebration of her marriage to Matthew, 4th Earl of Lennox – and of sacred and profane love in general. This is a supreme example, allowing us a glimpse into the splendour of the Renaissance court in all its finery.

1 The brooch given by Mary to her companion Mary Seton.

2 The Penicuik Necklace, made from jewellery given by Mary to her servant Giles Mowbray.

3 The 'Ermine portrait' of Elizabeth I, in which she wears the black pearls stolen from Mary by Regent Moray and sold to her.

43

1561

The Return of the Native

Mary's years at the heart of the French royal court had provided little preparation for the difficulties that would face her at home. With no mother to advise her, she would be compelled to place faith in a variety of nobles and other counsellors who could only be relied upon if their own interests were served. Principal among these was her elder half-brother, Lord James.

She had been well trained in the pleasures and trappings of royal life. She was highly educated, with sophisticated tastes. What she conspicuously lacked was experience of the cut and thrust of political life. In her absence, factions of nobles had struggled for power, and her mother, who had eventually claimed the regency in 1554, had been ruthlessly overthrown. The loyalty and support of her senior subjects could not be taken for granted.

A key driver of social instability had been religious reform. The unrest that was already being felt in France had also divided Scotland, though it had theoretically been resolved by the Reformation Parliament of August 1560. Scotland was now Protestant; Mary remained Catholic.

There was also an ambiguous relationship with the English court. Mary's dealings with her cousin Queen Elizabeth were amicable, if cautious and remote. However, Elizabeth's chief advisor, Sir William Cecil, saw Mary as a profound threat, and largely devoted his career to her downfall.

None of this was an easy prospect for a queen who was only 18 years old.

▶ Mary's arrival at Leith in August 1561, as depicted in an engraving of the 1800s.

1561

19 August
Lamb's House, Leith, Edinburgh
Terra firma

As residents of Edinburgh know, the term 'summer' can be misleading. It was early on a damp, cold, misty late-summer morning that Mary made landfall at the port of Leith, two miles north-east of Edinburgh. This was her first sight of her native land in more than 12 years. Perhaps her sense of purpose overcame the gloomy climatic conditions.

It had been an unusually brisk passage from Calais, lasting only five days, and Mary's prompt arrival took Scotland somewhat by surprise. Her ship's captain, Nicolas de Villegagnon, had to fire its guns to attract a crowd.

Mary's first step was to rest for an hour or so and refresh herself. For this purpose, the royal party repaired to the home of a wealthy merchant, Andrew Lamb, a grand mansion tucked into the back streets near Leith shore.

Lamb's House was perhaps the finest in Leith; however, the building that now bears that name dates from the early 1600s, and must be a replacement for – or a modification of – the one visited by Mary.

In 2010 it was purchased by the local architect Nicholas Groves-Raines. It has now been refurbished as private housing and offices, with many of its period features preserved or restored.

At the time of Mary's arrival, Leith was Scotland's main port. It had many links with royalty. Most recently, it had been the stronghold where Mary of Guise had held out with her French forces.

Mary was to become an important figure in the port. In 1566 she confirmed the right of the Incorporation of Masters and Mariners to collect the Prime Gilt, a tax on imports arriving in Leith. This was used to fund the activities of Trinity House, a charity that supported indigent retired sailors and the families of those lost at sea, as well as commissioning lighthouses and providing training for navigators.

The present Trinity House, built in 1816–18, stands on the vaults of a hospital built by the Incorporation in Mary of Guise's time. The perimeter wall still includes a carved stone plaque dated 1555. Now a museum, it houses an eclectic collection of maritime artefacts and numerous paintings, including an unusual one of Mary.

	1561 31 January	19 August
⧗	The Edict of Orléans suspends persecution of the Huguenots in France.	Mary arrives at Leith, near Edinburgh.

1 A portrait of Mary, which hangs at Trinity House Maritime Museum in Leith.

2 Lamb's House, Leith. The existing structure dates to the early 1600s, and was extensively refurbished in 2008–13, but it probably stands on the site where Mary rested after disembarking.

24 August
Palace of Holyroodhouse, Edinburgh
Critical Mass

Mary came home a year after Parliament had adopted a Reformed confession of faith, effectively establishing Scotland as a Protestant nation. She was, and would always remain, a Catholic, and religion would become a key issue.

She reached Holyrood a few hours after landing at Leith. This would be her main residence throughout her reign, but she had never been here before. Her apartments were in the north-west tower, built as royal accommodation by her father, James V. They have been preserved largely unchanged and may still be visited.

The palace was a sprawling complex. The gateway was arched and turreted; inside, the approach to the palace was flanked by formal gardens. Arthur's Seat and the Salisbury Crags loomed just to the south.

Mary's voyage from France had been remarkably swift, but her baggage train was being carried on more sluggish vessels and had not yet arrived. The palace rooms would not have been completely bare, but they would certainly have seemed bleak compared to the voluptuous splendour of French royal châteaux, and none of Mary's exquisite furniture and wall hangings were yet in place. These rooms must also have carried poignant reminders of their previous occupant, Mary's late mother Mary of Guise.

On Sunday 24 August, she attended Mass, as she had done every Sunday since early childhood.

Through negotiation with her Protestant half-brother, Lord James, she had secured acceptance of this practice.

But not everyone was tolerant. As the queen worshipped in her private chapel, Patrick, Master of Lindsay – an ally of the Protestant figurehead John Knox – arrived with a group of followers. They created a disturbance in the palace courtyard, calling for the priest to be murdered. A servant was molested and his candles and other accoutrements of Catholic worship were 'trodden in the mire'.

The following day, Mary issued a stern declaration that her servants were not to be harassed in any way, and that she intended to put an end to the trouble between Catholics and Protestants. If only it were that simple.

3 The Palace of Holyroodhouse, with the royal apartments in the north-west tower at the left. A mirror image of this structure was added to the palace for Charles II in the 1670s.

PALATIVM REGIVM EDINENSE
quod & Cænobium S. Crucis
The royal palace of holy rood house. by J.C

1561

Edinburgh Castle and the Royal Mile
Homecoming queen

The response to Mary's arrival in Scotland had been muted, partly because she had made such a swift crossing from France. But her time at the French court had taught her the value of spectacle. She was eager to mark her return and greet her subjects in some style.

On 31 August, the Provost of Edinburgh had hosted a banquet for the queen and the party who had accompanied her from France. This was held at the former residence of Cardinal Beaton, on Blackfriars Wynd.

By Tuesday 2 September she was ready to celebrate her arrival like a true Renaissance monarch. She slipped out of Holyrood on horseback, skirted around the city, and made her way up the hill to Edinburgh Castle. After a state banquet in the great hall, she had the castle fire its guns.

There followed a parade down the Royal Mile, the main street connecting Edinburgh Castle to Holyrood. The citizenry crowded the streets, where the town council had laid on various forms of pageantry. Just below the castle at Castlehill, Mary and her accompanying nobles were joined by a procession of 50 young men dressed as Moors, in yellow costumes with black hats and masks.

◄ An artist's impression of Mary's grand entrance to Edinburgh. For most citizens, the first sight of their queen for 13 years was cause for celebration, but there were dissenters.

A little further down, at the Lawnmarket, the procession passed under a brightly coloured triumphal arch, to the accompaniment of a choir of children. Here, a little boy descended on a rope from a mechanical cloud. He handed her the keys to the city, a bible and a psalter. This, however, was a pointed gesture: these were symbols of Protestant worship.

Passing St Giles Cathedral, Mary came to the Tolbooth. Here there was a dumbshow of four virgins representing Fortitude, Justice, Temperance and Prudence.

At the Salt Tron – a public weighscales – an overtly rebellious presentation had been prepared. It was to show a Catholic priest being burned at the altar during Mass. The Earl of Huntly, who was leading the procession, put a stop to this, and three Jews were hastily substituted for the priest, pleasing both Catholics and Protestants.

Finally, at the Netherbow, the eastern entrance to the city, a papier mâché dragon was set on fire. To Protestant eyes, this powerful beast may have represented the Pope; and by this point Mary must have been aware of a seditious undercurrent to the celebrations.

Despite this, the crowd was largely benign and welcoming. Mary may have been stung by the Protestant provocations, but she had the wisdom not to over-react. She had witnessed the corrosive sectarian divide in France, which would soon succumb to religious war. She decided to take the bull by the horns, and summoned John Knox, figurehead of the Scottish Reformation, to Holyrood.

The school of hard Knox

The debates over religion between Mary and John Knox are the stuff of legend. Beginning at Holyrood on 4 September 1561, they took place over years and in various locations. The most complete record of these discussions was written by Knox himself.

Knox had already shown his colours in his notorious book, *The First Blast of the Trumpet against the Monstrous Regimen of Women* (1558) whose main targets were Mary of Guise and the Catholic Mary I of England. Women were unfit to govern, he had argued, 'For their sight ... is but blindness: their strength, weakness: their counsel, foolishness: and judgement, frenzy.' He had taken a similarly dim view of 'idolatrous' (i.e. Catholic) men.

But Knox did not want to underplay this new adversary's intelligence and spirit — where would be the victory in that? He embraced a rather cheerless doctrine, but his prose is vigorous and vivid.

At this first meeting, Mary accused him of fomenting rebellion against her and against her mother, of writing 'against her just authority', of provoking bloodshed in England and of attracting accusations of witchcraft.

Knox's riposte, in his own account, includes a resigned offer of compliance. He likens his predicament to that of the apostle St Paul. 'I have communicated my judgement to the world; if the realm finds no inconveniency in the regimen of a woman, that which they approve shall I not farther disallow, than within my own breast, but shall be as well content to live under your grace as Paul was to live under [the Roman emperor] Nero. And my hope is, that so long as that ye defile not your hands with the blood of the saints of God, that neither I nor that book shall either hurt you or your authority.'

A grudging respect almost certainly existed between them, but no resolution was possible. Mary was devoutly Catholic and sought a tolerance that Knox's stripe of Protestantism could not allow.

▲ A contemporary woodcut shows Mary debating with Knox and with the exiled English church reformer Christopher Goodman.

Food and feasting had been an integral part of kingship for centuries. As far back as the early medieval period (probably even into prehistoric times), the provision and consumption of food was an important part of fostering and cementing relationships between lords and their followers. This continued into the later medieval and early modern periods.

1

Eating was an important manifestation of the social order. How much food you were entitled to, what you ate and where you were permitted to eat it were all symbolic. Famine was still a constant threat, so even being able to choose food rather than eat whatever was available was a significant way of displaying wealth and status.

At meals, those of the highest status received the greatest variety of dishes directly from the kitchen. Even as a captive in England, Mary routinely sat down twice a day to two courses of at least 15 dishes each – a staggering total of 60 different dishes per day.

However, the 'leftovers' of these dishes were passed down to those of lower ranks, so the number and variety of dishes is not as extravagant or wasteful as first appears.

This demarcation was considered important enough to pass legislation to preserve it. For example, on 1 February 1552, how much meat people of different ranks should be allowed was described in an Act of Parliament.

Archbishops, bishops and earls could have eight dishes of meat, barons and freeholders four, and burgesses and other 'substantial' men three.

There were fines for breaking the rules, but also exceptions such as Easter, Christmas, marriages and banquets for foreigners. (After the Reformation, the Protestant Church of Scotland tried to discourage feasts associated with religious ceremonies.) This was not the only attempt to control what people ate, which suggests not everyone adhered to the rules. This is unsurprising: who would wish to advertise themselves as being of lower status?

The cost of providing food could be very high, especially as hospitality was an important custom throughout Scotland. Conspicuous consumption was a crucial part of lordly display and it was important to provide appropriate sustenance for guests.

This was advantageous for those with the ability to travel. As well as providing the opportunity to see and be seen, Mary's frequent progresses transferred the burden of feeding the court from her own pocket to those of her lords. Mary was fortunate that her French income covered many of her household costs, but being frequently entertained by her lords no doubt made the money go further.

Mary's position as queen gave her another advantage when meeting the often massive costs of appropriate display. She could seek a grant of tax from Parliament to cover the costs – though she only did this once, for Prince James's baptism (see page 82).

FOOD AND FEASTING

1 A red deer stag. Mary greatly enjoyed hunting, but venison was also one of the many locally produced foods supplied to the court.

2

Others wishing to squander beyond their means often incurred huge debts to meet the social pressures to spend. The baptism was obviously a major political occasion as well as a personal celebration. It highlights the propaganda uses to which such occasions could be put. Coming just nine months after Rizzio's murder (see page 74), it was a perfect opportunity for Mary to re-establish her political position.

The baptism was a special case, though, and arrangements for eating, serving and so on would have been very different for day-to-day meals. A description of the Rizzio murder, for instance, has Mary eating in private, with only a few courtiers in attendance. This was probably the most usual arrangement, with other high-ranking guests also dining separately from the majority of the court and staff eating near or within their place of work. The main meal was usually eaten around midday, but banquets were generally held in the evening.

Much of the produce consumed at court could be provided directly from the extensive royal estates and parks around the country. Herbs, freshwater fish and venison were among the products supplied directly to the household, while other consumables could be imported or purchased locally. Bread and beer would either be bought locally or produced onsite: most noble residences would include a brewhouse and bakehouse. Fine white bread was the most prestigious kind.

Weak beer was normally drunk by the lower ranks instead of water, which was more likely to carry diseases. The elite preferred imported fine wine, though they undoubtedly consumed beer as well, depending on the occasion and circumstances.

In general, the diet would not be considered very healthy by modern standards, and must have contributed to the much lower life expectancy enjoyed by people of all ranks at the time.

2 An artist's impression of the wedding feast Mary attended at Castle Campbell in January 1563.

1562-4

Progresses and Setbacks

The early years of Mary's personal reign were challenging, but not without successes. Her personal charm helped her gain allegiance from her nobles – even some of those who had overthrown her mother. But there were many obstacles to stability.

During this period, Mary's focus was largely on two issues. The first was the difficulty of maintaining religious tolerance, with devoted Protestants on one side, and on the other Catholics praying fervently for counter-reformation.

The second was securing her claim to the English throne. As the legitimate great-granddaughter of Henry VII of England, she was positioned to succeed her first cousin once removed, Elizabeth I, who now seemed unlikely to produce an heir. Moreover, Elizabeth was considered illegitimate by all Catholics and many Protestants.

Diplomacy between the two queens continued over years, and in 1561 a meeting between them had seemed likely. But Elizabeth, understandably, was wary of her cousin.

▶ The elegant gatehouse of Falkland Palace, added by Mary's father James V.

Throughout her personal reign, Mary spent most of her time at Holyrood, but she also travelled a great deal. Her movements around the country were for various purposes: to appear at state occasions, to attend to political business and sit in judicial courts, to attend weddings and social occasions, and to rest and enjoy herself. Vacating the royal palaces also allowed them to be cleaned – no small matter in an age before running water.

A key purpose of travel was the royal progress: a recognised means of meeting subjects – or at least seeing and being seen by them – and fostering their loyalty. Royal progresses were also practised by Elizabeth I, but the need for visibility was perhaps greater in Scotland, where power was much less centralised. This was partly because a succession of child monarchs had boosted the power of nobles such as the Earl of Arran, who had governed the country during Mary's minority.

Aside from her royal residences, Mary stayed in many kinds of accommodation. Often, she was the guest of a monastery; at other times she stayed with noblemen, lairds or burgesses.

She was a costly houseguest – indeed, a secondary purpose of a progress was to alleviate pressure on the royal household's resources, consuming local produce. However, it was a great honour to accommodate this charismatic queen, and her hosts had the chance to influence her opinion and petition her for favours. There is some evidence that those who had hosted her tended to remain loyal in later years.

Mary travelled mainly on horseback. Although her mother had introduced the first coach to Scotland, most thoroughfares were unsuitable for vehicles. She was an accomplished horsewoman, and had brought her favourite horses with her from France.

She also travelled by water. When visiting Fife, she crossed the Firth of Forth via the Queen's Ferry (established by Queen Margaret in the 11th century, to provide access to Dunfermline Abbey). On progress in 1563, she visited the west coast, travelling via the Firth of Clyde.

Her travels were not always eventful, but they certainly exposed her to sights – and people – never seen in the rarefied confines of the royal court.

1562

11 January
Crichton Castle, Midlothian
Midwinter revels

1 Crichton Castle, principal seat of the Hepburn family.

A wedding celebration brought Mary into contact again with the Earl of Bothwell, the roguish nobleman who would ultimately be her third husband.

Mary travelled little in the first few months of her personal reign, though she did make a brief progress in September 1561. On that trip, she paid nostalgic visits to her childhood homes at Stirling and Linlithgow, also taking in Dundee, Perth and St Andrews. (At Stirling, on 13 or 14 September, she nearly perished when a candle set light to her bed curtains. The English ambassador Thomas Randolph noted, with some disappointment, that an ancient prophecy had been wrong to predict a queen's death by burning at Stirling.)

In January 1562, Mary braved the winter weather to visit Crichton Castle, 12 miles south-east of Edinburgh. The occasion was one she would not have wanted to miss. She very much enjoyed weddings, and was generous with gifts. And this was the marriage celebration of John Stewart, secular prior of Coldingham, a half-brother she held in particular affection.

The wedding was held at Crichton because it was the birthplace and family seat of the bride, Janet Hepburn. She was the sister of the swashbuckling admiral James Hepburn, 4th Earl of Bothwell. The groom was also a notorious figure at court, known for his 'leaping and dancing'. The previous month, he and Bothwell had become embroiled in a street brawl in Edinburgh, which resulted in Bothwell's expulsion from the city.

Little more than two years previously, in November 1559, Bothwell's activities had led to mayhem at Crichton itself. Acting on behalf of Mary of Guise, he had intercepted 4,000 crowns sent by Elizabeth I, intended to support the rebellious Lords of the Congregation. In response, 50 soldiers were sent to besiege the castle and made off with 'great spoil'. Bothwell's relationship with the Protestant lords would never recover.

On this chilly Sunday, however, those conflicts were forgotten as Mary, Lord James Stewart and the other guests celebrated with good cheer the marriage of her favourite half-brother. Sadly, he was to die less than two years later.

1562 1 March	May–October	22 September	28 October
At the **Massacre of Vassy**, 63 unarmed Huguenots are killed, and over 100 wounded, by troops of Francis, Duke of Guise. This is the first major event of the French Wars of Religion.	At the **Siege of Rouen** in northern France, Huguenots are driven out by Catholics.	**Treaty of Hampton Court** between Elizabeth I and the Huguenot leader Louis, Prince of Condé. Elizabeth agrees to send 3,000 English troops to occupy Le Havre and Dieppe, as well as offering economic aid.	At the **Battle of Corrichie** George Gordon, Earl of Huntly is defeated by Mary's half-brother Moray.

1562

25 August
Edzell Castle, Angus
Sitting in judgement

During her progress of 1562, Mary spent a night at Edzell Castle, the handsome residence of Sir David Lindsay, Lord of Edzell. While there, she took part in a criminal hearing with her privy council – her closest body of political advisers.

When in Edinburgh, Mary met her privy council almost daily. On progress, she convened with them less frequently, as needs and opportunities arose. The meeting at Edzell was probably held in the state rooms in the west range, completed around 1550. (The castle's splendid formal gardens were not laid out until 1604.)

Mary had chosen her privy council carefully. It was made up of 12 men, seven Protestant and five Catholic.

Unavoidably, they included some of the lords who had overthrown her mother. At its heart were her half-brother, Lord James, and two of his closest associates, James Douglas, Earl of Morton and William Maitland of Lethington, both major figures in Mary's life.

The Register of the Council shows that at Edzell, a certain Robert Montgomery was brought before the queen. He wished to lodge a formal complaint against John Fullarton of Kinnaber, whom he accused of 'falseing and feinyeinge' the stamp of an official messenger, fraudulently obtaining the sum of 500 marks. Montgomery ardently requested the queen's intervention, but her response is not recorded.

2 The west range of Edzell Castle, added around 1550, where Mary probably slept.

3 The arched gateway through the west range. The panels above would have held carved coats of arms, representing both the Lindsay family and the Scottish monarch.

Making progress

Mary undertook a number of progresses during her personal reign, staying in the following places:

11–29 September 1561
(North-east) Linlithgow, Stirling, Kincardine, Leslie, Perth, Dundee, St Andrews, Cupar, Falkland.

3 March–14 May 1562
(Fife) Dunfermline, Dysart, Durie, St Andrews, Cupar, Falkland, Cupar, St Andrews, Falkland, Lochleven.

11 August–22 November 1562
(North-east) Linlithgow, Falkirk, Stirling, Kincardine, Coupar Angus, Glamis, Edzell, Dunnottar, Aberdeen, Balquahain, Rothiemay, Castle of Grange, Balvenie, Elgin, Kinloss, Darnaway, Nairn, Inverness, Kilravock, Darnaway, Spynie, Boyne, Banff, Gight, Aberdeen, Craig, Bonnington, Kincardine, Arbroath, Dundee, Kilspindie, Perth, Tullibardine, Stirling, Linlithgow.

13 February–18 May 1563
(Fife) Dunfermline, Rossend, Falkland, St Andrews, Pitlothie, St Andrews, Cupar, Falkland, Ballinbreich, Naughton, Pitlothie, St Andrews, Falkland, Cupar, Newark, Falkland, Lochleven, Falkland, Newark, Cupar, St Andrews, Rossend.

1 July–7 September 1563
(South-west then south-east) Dumbarton, Hamilton, Glasgow, Dumbarton, Rossdhu, Dumbarton, Carrick, Thoard, Inverarary, Strachur, Dunoon, Toward, Southannan, Eglinton, Ayr, Dunure, Ardmillan, Ardstinchar, Glenluce, Whithorn, Clary, Kenmure, Kirkcudbright, St Mary's Isle, Terregles, Drumlanrig, Crawfordjohn, Cowthally, Skirling, Peebles, Borthwick, Dalhousie, Roslin, Craigmillar.

22 July–15 September 1564
(North-east; itinerary partly unknown) Linlithgow, Stirling, Kincardine, Blair (probably), Luncarty, Inverness, Gartly, Aberdeen, Dunottar, Dundee, St Andrews.

20 January–25 February 1565
(Fife) Falkland, Collairnie, Ballinbreich, St Andrews, Anstruther, Newark, St Andrews, Lundie, Wemyss, Balmutto.

1563 18 February	19 March	28 July	**1564** 23 April	27 May
Mary's uncle, Francis, Duke of Guise, is shot and fatally wounded.	**The Edict of Amboise** grants some religious toleration to the Huguenots, especially to aristocrats, officially ending the first War of Religion. Combined Huguenot and royal forces besiege the English in Le Havre.	**The English surrender** Le Havre.	**William Shakespeare** is born at Stratford-Upon-Avon. He is baptised on 26 April.	**John Calvin,** father of the Protestant doctrine of Calvinism, dies, aged 54 in Geneva.

1562

13 September
Inverness Castle
Trouble up north

As Mary progressed northwards, the weather grew grim. The English diplomat Thomas Randolph, who accompanied her, described it as 'extreme foul and cold'. These stormy conditions were apt for Mary's first major confrontation with a senior nobleman.

The problems began when her party reached Aberdeen on 27 August. They were greeted by George Gordon, 4th Earl of Huntly, his wife and 1,500 of his followers. Huntly had been specifically instructed to limit his retinue to 100.

The most powerful noble in the region, Huntly was a flighty and unreliable character, known as the Cock of the North. His nine sons were also renowned troublemakers. Sir John Gordon, for example, had scandalised Edinburgh with a catalogue of criminal violence, sexual impropriety and marital duplicity, and had recently escaped from jail. He now harboured ambitions to marry the queen.

A rift had grown between Mary and Huntly. In part, this was fallout from her diplomacy with Elizabeth. Huntly was a Catholic, and disliked the prospect of an alliance with Protestant England.

He was also resentful of Mary's half-brother, Lord James, an old rival whom she had recently appointed Earl of Mar and Earl of Moray. Having administered both earldoms for years on behalf of the Crown, Huntly felt they were rightfully his.

Mary spent a few nights in Aberdeen, then toured the region, stopping for two nights in the handsome new apartments of her privy councillor John Stewart, Earl of Atholl, at Balvenie Castle. She proceeded to Inverness, pointedly bypassing Huntly's castle of Strathbogie (now Huntly Castle).

It was at Inverness Castle that Mary encountered open rebellion. The captain, another Gordon, refused to admit her. Mary was furious. She spent the night nearby and returned with an army of local clansmen. After a siege of two or three days, they captured the castle and hanged Gordon from the battlements.

Huntly, meanwhile, was lurking at Strathbogie. As Mary returned across the Spey, Sir John appeared with a force of 1,000 men, aiming to kidnap her. But Mary had 3,000 men, and on seeing them the rebels fled.

Mary's blood was up, and Randolph was impressed. 'I never saw her merrier, never dismayed, nor never thought that stomach to be in her that I find,' he wrote. The Cock of the North's days were numbered.

28 October 1562
The Battle of Corrichie

On 16 October, Huntly and his son Sir John were 'put to the horn' — declared outlaw. Huntly had been slipping from stronghold to stronghold, avoiding Mary's forces, and only narrowly evaded capture at Strathbogie. His wife, the redoubtable Countess Elizabeth, tried to secure an interview with the queen. When that failed, she urged her husband to assert himself by martial force.

Though elderly and overweight, Huntly gamely raised an army 800 or so strong and marched towards Aberdeen. He drew up his men on the Hill of Fare above Corrichie, assuring them they were fearsome enough to provoke desertion among Mary's troops. He then knelt to pray: 'O Lord I have been a bloodthirsty man, and by my means has mekle [much] innocent blood been spilt; but Thou give me victory this day and I shall serve Thee all the days of my life.'

Mary had made her own preparations: her men were armed with cannon and harquebus — portable, tripod-fired guns. When they took up position at the foot of the hill, these weapons helped drive Huntly's men off the slopes into boggy marshland. Many were killed. Huntly, Sir John and another son, Adam Gordon of Auchindoun, were captured.

At this point, Huntly suffered a seizure, 'burst and swelled' and died on the spot. On 2 November, Sir John was beheaded at Aberdeen, a bloody spectacle Mary was compelled to watch, which upset her deeply.

1 The City of Inverness in an illustration of the 1690s, with the castle at the right.

17–19 September

Spynie Palace, Moray
The mating bishop

2 The coat of arms of Patrick Hepburn, Bishop of Moray.

3 David's Tower, the bishop's grand residence at Spynie.

While contemplating how to tackle Huntly, Mary sought refuge at Spynie Palace, north of Elgin. This was the grand fortified residence of Patrick Hepburn, Bishop of Moray – a powerful magnate of the Church.

Hepburn had been appointed to the bishopric in 1538, the year Mary's parents were married, and held it until 1571. His coat of arms can still be seen on the wall of David's Tower, the massive five-storey residential building where Mary would probably have been accommodated.

2

Hepburn was known for enjoying a luxurious lifestyle, and for neglecting his duties, both spiritual and political, to the region he controlled. During Mary's childhood, he was a member of Regent Arran's privy council, but he seems to have devoted most of his energies to the pursuit of pleasure.

According to the contemporary chronicler, Robert Lindsay of Pitscottie, he 'was a whoremaster all his days and committed whoredom and adultery both with maidens and men's wives'. He had at least 13 children to show for it, and went to some lengths to get most of them legitimised.

Like many of the churchmen of his day, Hepburn made a show of embracing the Reformation. He introduced some changes to worship at Elgin Cathedral, but at heart he seems to have been a rather lax Catholic. He ultimately forfeited his title, but was allowed to stay on at Spynie until his death in 1573.

Fortunately, Mary had not come to him for spiritual advice. She was here on progress, and to plot the come-uppance of Huntly.

Bothwell's Visits

The Bishop of Moray was a kinsman of James Hepburn, 4th Earl of Bothwell, the dashing nobleman who would eventually marry the queen. Bothwell had spent part of his childhood in the comfortable surroundings of Spynie.

He cannot have felt quite so carefree when he paid his last visit to Spynie, seeking refuge after the Battle of Carberry in 1567. With typical bravado, he pre-empted an assassination attempt, killing one of the bishop's sons in the process. He soon slipped away to Shetland, where he made another daring escape to Norway, before finally being captured and imprisoned in Denmark.

Habeas corpse

George Gordon, 4th Earl of Huntly, died quite literally in the saddle — he suffered his seizure while on horseback at Corrichie. But death did not prevent him from being put on trial. His body was disembowelled, embalmed and taken to Edinburgh, where, in May 1563, it stood trial in an upright coffin. Huntly was convicted of treason and forfeited of his estates.

3

1563

9–12 January

Castle Campbell, Clackmannanshire
Dollar bells

Another winter wedding took Mary to Castle Campbell, the handsome lowland seat of the earls of Argyll, sited above the lush, dramatic precipices of Dollar Glen.

The match this time was between a distant cousin, James Stewart, Lord Doune, and Margaret, sister of the 5th Earl of Argyll. This was a powerful alliance and probably had a political element, but Argyll seems to have thrown a good party. During one pastoral masque, the guests dressed up as shepherds in white damask and played lutes. Mary was keen on fancy dress, and a skilled lutenist, so one can imagine her enjoying herself. However, her relationship with the earl was not always cordial.

Of royal descent, the earls of Argyll were among the most powerful nobles in Scotland, controlling a huge swathe of territory in the west. Archibald Campbell, 4th Earl, had been a senior participant at Mary's coronation, carrying the Sword of State.

Towards the end of his life he developed Protestant leanings, and in about 1556, he invited John Knox to preach at Castle Campbell. Knox is said to have used a small rocky promontory below the terraced gardens as a natural pulpit.

In 1558, the 4th Earl died and was succeeded by his son, also Archibald, who was unhappily married to Jean Stewart, one of Mary's half-sisters.

The 5th Earl was a committed Protestant and had been among the Lords of the Congregation who overthrew Mary of Guise and negotiated the Treaty of Edinburgh. However, he was among the party escorting Mary to Holyrood following her arrival at Leith in 1561, and she soon recruited him to her privy council.

After Mary's marriage to Darnley in 1565, which he boycotted, Argyll joined her brother the Earl of Moray in rebellion. During the Chaseabout Raid which followed, Mary did not return to Castle Campbell, but she passed close by and received its surrender.

The 5th Earl would play a crucial (and disastrous) role at the Battle of Langside, Mary's last stand in Scotland.

▶ Castle Campbell in midwinter.

An honoured guest

Mary enjoyed weddings, and always attended them if she could. She was generous with presents, and often paid for the celebrations. When Bothwell married Jean Gordon of Huntly in February 1566, Mary paid for a glorious wedding dress of cloth of silver, and an extravagant wedding banquet after the ceremony. Even the day after Darnley's murder in February 1567 she appeared at the wedding of her bedchamber woman Margaret Carwood to her distant cousin John Stuart, having paid for the dress and the banquet.

▶ James Hepburn, Earl of Bothwell, and his wife Jean Gordon of Huntly. He would later divorce her to marry Mary.

John Knox: marriage guidance counsellor

In April 1563, Mary asked John Knox to intervene in the troubled marriage of her half-sister Jean to Archibald Campbell, 5th Earl of Argyll. Jean Stewart was a capricious young woman who preferred the excitement of Edinburgh to the seclusion of Argyll, and tongues at court were wagging. According to Knox's account, Mary told him that Argyll, 'treats her not in many things so honestly as I think ye yourself would require'.

On 7 May 1563, Knox composed a cautionary letter to Argyll, advising: 'Your behaviour toward your wife is very offensive ... Every moment of that filthy pleasure ... shall be the occasion and cause of everlasting damnation, unless you speedily repent ... Sin, my lord, is sweet in drinking, but in digesting more bitter than the gall.'

The couple were temporarily reconciled, but divorced in 1573. For his own part, Knox provoked scandal in 1564 when he married his second wife, Margaret Stewart, 33 years his junior.

1563

Rossend Castle, Fife
The misfortunes
of Châtelard

Mary's story is often described in terms of its romance and its tragedy. But even she is rivalled in those areas by the hapless poet Pierre de Bocosel de Châtelard.

He had been among the French retinue accompanying Mary on her return from France in 1561. He was handsome, well-dressed and refined, a gifted poet and a skilful exponent of the kind of elaborate flattery that a beautiful young queen could expect to receive from her courtiers. For Mary this was pleasing, but probably nothing more. Châtelard, however, seems to have been more earnest than his writing style suggested.

After returning to France, he reappeared in Scotland the following autumn, and presented Mary with a book of his poems. Mary, charmed but still well within the bounds of propriety, reciprocated by giving him a horse and some spending money for clothes. (Knox, characteristically, cast this as compelling evidence of a sinful liaison.)

On progress in Fife, Mary spent one night at Rossend Castle overlooking the Firth of Forth. (The castle's most famous feature is its painted ceiling, dating from Mary's era.) It was here that Châtelard seized the chance to slip into her chamber and hide under her bed. He was soon discovered, thrown out and banished from court.

The incident might have been quietly forgotten, but Châtelard's ardour overwhelmed his good sense and he followed Mary to St Andrews.

Two nights later, he burst into her bedchamber as she was disrobing and attempted a hasty seduction. The shrieks of Mary and her handmaidens soon brought rescue. Châtelard was personally apprehended by the Earl of Moray. In her shock Mary demanded his execution there and then, but Moray calmed her.

Châtelard stood trial a few days later. His defence was unconvincing. The first intrusion, he explained, had been brought about by a sudden need to sleep; the second had merely been an attempt to explain the first.

He was convicted of treason and executed at St Andrews a week later. On the scaffold, he recited movingly from his mentor, the poet Ronsard, Mary's former tutor. He then bade 'Adieu' to 'the most cruel princess of the world'.

It is ironic that Châtelard's initial indiscretion took place on St Valentine's Day, a festival associated with romantic love from at least the 1380s.

1 Rossend Castle today.

2 A Victorian engraving shows Châtelard wooing Mary with his lute.

1563

9–11 August
Glenluce Abbey/ Whithorn Priory, Galloway
A pilgrim's progress

Mary's grandfather, James IV, famously made a number of long pilgrimages, to Tain in the north-east and Whithorn in the south-west. Mary would have been conscious of treading in his footsteps as she visited Whithorn. But the varied fortunes of local clerics spoke loudly of changed times.

On 9 August, Mary stayed at Glenluce Abbey, a grand medieval monastery of the Cistercian order near Luce Bay. By the time of her visit, the abbey was under the secular management of Gilbert Kennedy, 4th Earl of Cassilis, and he was Mary's host.

However, 10 monks were still in residence, under the leadership of Abbot Thomas Hay. In the 1550s, Hay had successfully fought a legal case against the Lord of Lochinvar, over occupation of the abbey, and Cassilis had allowed him to stay on. Glenluce is now largely ruined, but its ornate chapter house – or meeting room – survives in good condition.

The following day, Mary rode 20 miles to Whithorn, where she slept. Closely associated with St Ninian, Whithorn was among the earliest Christian establishments in Scotland. It was a major focus for pilgrimage over many centuries.

The Prior of Whithorn at the time of Mary's visit was Malcolm Fleming, son of the Earl of Wigtown. He would have been her host, had he not been imprisoned that May for celebrating Mass.

On 11 August, Mary stayed nearby at Clary, the bishop of Whithorn's palace, but at this time there was no bishop of Whithorn.

The post had been held in 1558–60 by Alexander Gordon, but in 1560, he had renounced Catholicism to join the Reformed Kirk. John Knox was delighted: Gordon was the most senior churchman to convert.

Despite this, the Protestant General Assembly removed him from office in June 1562 until such time as 'the Kirks of Galloway craved him'. Six years later, he was banned from 'any function in the Kirk'.

The travails of these churchmen serve to illustrate the realities of religious life in the years after the Reformation.

3 The royal coat of arms on the vennel leading to Whithorn Priory.

4 Mary's grandfather, James IV, who made several pilgrimages to Whithorn.

1564

Around 15 August
Beauly Priory, near Inverness
A place of beauty

On the second of her two progresses in the north-east, Mary stopped at Beauly, a priory established for monks of the Valliscaulian order around 1230. The monks were allowed to stay on after the Reformation, and would still have been here in Mary's day.

The surroundings are particularly attractive, and the charter, written in Latin, names the new establishment as Monasterium de Bello Loco – 'Monastery of the beautiful place' – from which the name Beauly derives.

When Mary visited, she famously confirmed this opinion in French: *'Oui, c'est un beau lieu.'* ('Yes, it is a beatiful place.')

The Valliscaulians took their name from the place near Dijon, France, where they were founded: Val-des-Choux. It also translates rather charmingly, as 'Valley of the Cabbages'. Only three Valliscaulian monasteries were ever established in Britain, all in the Scottish Highlands.

5 Beauly Priory: 'a beautiful place'.

By all accounts – even those of the eternally disapproving John Knox – Mary was a remarkably energetic woman. Her personality was gregarious; she was constantly talking, arguing, crying, and laughing. Similarly, she loved physical activity, and took up many opportunities to participate in recreation.

Many of her activities were those expected of Renaissance ladies. She took delight in being outdoors, whether it was to walk, ride or hunt. She went almost everywhere on horseback, famously riding at the head of her army during the Chaseabout Raid: a picture of youthful majesty.

Mary's love of horses and riding had begun in France. When she left Scotland, she was too young to hunt, but had watched proceedings with interest and excitement. Before long she wrote to her mother requesting some Shetland ponies, on which she and the other children at the French court could learn to ride.

She also learned the art of falconry, using her own pet falcon, and astonished the ladies of the court with her fearlessness and skill. When she began to hunt, aged 12 or 13, she rode with breeches under her skirts – a fashion Catherine de' Medici brought with her from Florence – allowing her to ride astride rather than side-saddle. This later scandalised the Scottish Calvinists.

Archery, falconry and hare coursing were popular activities of the day, and Mary was an enthusiastic participant. Hunting was also among her favourite pursuits, and a regular activity of the royal court. In 1564, the Earl of Atholl organised a great hunt in honour of the queen at Glen Tilt near Blair Castle. During the hunt, a grand total of 360 deer and five wolves were killed, although an eyewitness account mentions also that several Highlanders were wounded, and two or three killed outright, when a frightened stag charged at the hunters.

Some of Mary's leisure activities were similar to those of today. She often played real tennis at Falkland. The tennis court – or cachespule – in the palace grounds was built in 1539 for James V, and still survives, the world's oldest real tennis court. It is thought there was also one at Stirling.

Mary is rumoured to have played golf on links by the Firth of Forth, though we have no real evidence of this. Her detractors accused her of playing golf shortly after Darnley's assassination, indicating the insincerity of her grief. The source of this seems to be George Buchanan's description of her stay at Seton Palace, during which, he notes, she played sports in the surrounding fields which were 'clearly unsuitable for women'.

That account may be dubious, but it is on record that while in captivity in Carlisle Castle, she was permitted to watch a game of football played by the men of her retinue. A leather ball, encasing an inflated pig's bladder, was found behind a panel in what may have been her bedroom at Stirling Castle. Dated to the 1540s, this is the oldest known football in the world.

Mary also enjoyed 'biles', or billiards. During their courtship in 1565, Mary and Darnley played the game with another unwed couple, Mary Beaton and the English ambassador Thomas Randolph. Mary and Darnley together lost an agate ring and brooch worth 50 crowns. Other indoor pursuits that she participated in included backgammon and chess.

1

PASTIMES AND PLEASURES

Mary's library included *The Rules of Chess*, translated from French by William Caxton in 1474. She loved to watch puppet shows, a new fashion which had lately spread from Italy.

Above all other pursuits, however, Mary loved to dance. For this she was applauded on the Continent and criticised in Scotland. As a young woman in France she showed real flair. She was agile and expressive in her movements – so much so that her future father-in-law, Henry II, went to great lengths to find an Italian dance master for her. When she reached Scotland, she would dance with her Four Maries every night, sometimes until after midnight. While for many this liveliness in the Scottish court was an aspect of Mary's glamour, to the Protestants it was a marked sign of Mary's Catholic 'depravity'. John Knox described it as 'the vanity of the unfaithful'.

Mary also enjoyed singing, playing and listening to music. Her personal male servants were all musicians as well. She had a consort of five viol players and three lutenists.

This was how David Rizzio came to enter her service; when a trio of singing valets needed a bass to sing the fourth part, Rizzio left his post at the Savoyard court to work for her. She herself played the virginals, the clavichord and the clarsach or harp, and often sang while accompanying herself on the lute. Musicians would play to the court, as well as at grand balls and masques, or theatrical performances. At these events, Mary and her courtiers would dress in elaborate costumes and watch and perform tableaux for the company.

The passion that sustained Mary most in her later years was embroidery. Trained during her childhood in France, Mary loved sewing, and later often worked at her designs during official meetings. It was this activity that occupied her during her long years of captivity, and provided an outlet for her wit and humour when more physical exercise was denied her.

3

2

1 A leather football found at Stirling Castle, thought to be the oldest in the world.

2 An Edwardian illustration shows Mary playing golf at St Andrews.

3 A decorated clarsach given by Mary to Beatrix Gardyn of Banchory.

1565

The Long Lad

In the mid-1540s, Henry VIII had sent his armies into Scotland, aiming to secure by this 'Rough Wooing' a marriage between the infant Mary and his son Prince Edward. Twenty years later, Mary was an adult, a reigning queen, a widow, charming, attractive, wealthy, sophisticated and infinitely marriageable. Moreover, it was expected of her that she would produce an heir. The question of her marriage had become pressing.

Her hand was not a gift to be bestowed lightly. Scotland's position north of England gave it huge strategic importance. It had recently adopted Protestantism, but many of its people, including the queen herself and several leading nobles, were still Catholic. So a counter-reformation was certainly imaginable.

Various candidates had already been put forward. One was the Protestant James Hamilton, 3rd Earl of Arran, son of the former Regent Arran. This was not a new proposal, but dated from Mary's infancy. It had recently been revived by his ambitious father, who had also attempted to marry him to Elizabeth I. However, the earl was declared insane in 1562 and spent most of his life in confinement.

Another strong contender had been Charles of Asturias (known as Don Carlos), son of King Philip II of Spain. Although seven years Mary's junior, he would have brought Scotland into a powerful alliance with Catholic Spain. He had briefly been betrothed to Mary's childhood companion Elisabeth Valois, who for diplomatic reasons married his father instead. He too became mentally unstable in 1562, having suffered serious head injuries falling down a flight of stairs.

A more recent – if reluctant – candidate had been Robert Dudley, Earl of Leicester, a handsome English Protestant who was well known to be a favourite of Elizabeth I – perhaps even her lover. Elizabeth saw him as a means of keeping tabs on Mary, and controlling her. She even envisaged the three of them living together in London. But Mary was not persuaded.

The man who would eventually claim her hand was a young Englishman of Scottish descent, a cousin both of Mary and of Elizabeth I, with a strong dynastic claim to the English throne. Henry Stewart, Lord Darnley also happened to be tall, slender, cultured and strikingly good-looking. Elizabeth herself had admiringly dubbed him the 'long lad'.

Their marriage secured the Stuart claim to the English throne, and produced the child who would become king of both Scotland and England. But it was also disastrous, for Darnley and for Mary – the chief source of her troubles and the primary cause of her downfall.

▶ Henry Stewart, Lord Darnley, in a portrait attributed to Adrian Vanson. Vanson later became court painter to James VI.

1565

17 February
Wemyss Castle, Fife
Making eyes

1   Darnley and Mary together.
Their courtship was passionate,
but their marriage was disastrous.

2   A ryal coin minted in 1565 shows
Darnley and Mary as king and queen.
Only a few such coins were struck,
with two faces and his name given
before hers.

It was no chance meeting. Darnley had in fact been suggested as a suitor for Mary a few years earlier. But although the match between them had been devised for political purposes, it was not totally bereft of sexual chemistry.

Darnley's path to Mary's arms was paved by Elizabeth I. In 1564, she petitioned Mary to allow Darnley's father, the exiled Matthew Stewart, 4th Earl of Lennox, to return to Scotland. He had been banished for collaborating with the English during the Rough Wooing. Lennox soon charmed his way into Mary's inner circle, and his forfeited lands were eventually restored.

Meanwhile, Darnley had become a fixture at the English court, well known for his boyish good looks and mastery of the lute. More than this, he had royal Tudor blood – like Mary, he was a great-grandchild of Henry VII.

Elizabeth herself had proposed that Mary wed the Earl of Leicester, her favourite. Mary was willing to do so, on condition that Elizabeth named her as heir. When she refused, Darnley emerged as a better way to secure the English throne.

Towards the end of 1564, Mary had resolved to bring Darnley to Scotland; though she had not perhaps determined just yet to marry him. Soon afterwards, Elizabeth suddenly lost her nerve over the Leicester match, and granted Darnley a passport to travel to Scotland.

A meeting was arranged at the seat of Sir John Wemyss in Fife – a discreet venue, perhaps, for such a delicate encounter. (It was not quite their first meeting, however – Darnley had met Mary twice on visits to the French court as a teenage boy.)

One of those present, the diplomat Sir James Melville noted, 'Her Majesty took very well with him, and said, That he was the properest and best proportioned long Man that she had seen; for he was of a high Stature, long and small, even and straight.'

(Only a few months earlier, the same Melville had had this to say when Elizabeth probed him on Darnley's prospects: 'My answer was, That no woman of spirit would make choice of such a Man, who more resembled a Woman than a Man.')

Darnley and Mary stayed at Wemyss for two nights and took the same ferry back to Edinburgh. The courtship that had begun was swift and intense, aided by Mary's decision to nurse Darnley when he fell ill. Both parties clearly had ulterior motives, but it seems likely that a genuine passion was stirring.

1565

Palace of Holyroodhouse, Edinburgh
Repent at leisure

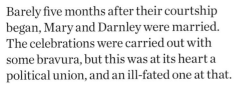

2

Barely five months after their courtship began, Mary and Darnley were married. The celebrations were carried out with some bravura, but this was at its heart a political union, and an ill-fated one at that.

Mary's choice of husband was not universally approved – though a match with universal approval was probably unachievable. Among the Scottish Protestant nobles it raised a fear of counter-reformation (though Darnley was far from devoutly Catholic, and liked to attend John Knox's sermons). More worryingly, if he became king they would be sidelined and perhaps worse. Moray refused to endorse his sister's marriage plans and was duly banished from court.

In London, Elizabeth and her chief adviser William Cecil took an equally dim view. Having attempted to exert control over Mary's marriage – and her eligibility to the English crown – they were being bypassed. Moreover, Cecil had convinced himself – and attempted to convince Elizabeth and her privy council – that the English people would switch their allegiance to a country with a royal couple at its helm.

Meanwhile, Darnley's father Lennox fostered support for the marriage, enlisting both Catholic and Protestant lords eager to further their own ambitions.

Chief among these was the Earl of Morton, a Moray ally, but also a cousin of Darnley's mother. He saw the match as a means of increasing his influence.

Philip II of Spain signalled his approval, as did Mary's former mother-in-law Catherine de' Medici in France, though she deceitfully expressed the opposite opinion to Elizabeth I. Diplomats and envoys were kept busy for months conveying urgent missives between heads of state and nobles.

Mary and Darnley, meanwhile, had been living it up together, mainly at Stirling Castle, stretching the bounds of propriety. When Darnley fell ill, Mary nursed him herself. But her devotion was misplaced.

Darnley was arrogant, dissolute and sexually licentious. He was a heavy drinker, his illness was probably syphilis, and he was rumoured to have dallied sexually with Mary's confidential secretary, David Rizzio. By the early summer, Mary was beginning to recognise the faults in his character, and she fell into an emotional slump. Nonetheless, she had made her decision, and she stuck to it defiantly – all the more so in the face of Elizabeth's disapproval.

The banns were read at St Giles Cathedral in Edinburgh on 22 July, and later that day Darnley was made Duke of Albany, a title reserved for royalty.

Mary petitioned Parliament to grant him the crown matrimonial, which would entitle him to reign in his own right in the event of her death. To his annoyance, Parliament refused, though he would still be called king after the wedding.

A week later, at the private chapel at Holyrood, they were married. Mary wore her white mourning robe, indicating she was a widow. Darnley placed three rings on her fingers, then knelt with her for prayers. Then he left, snubbing the wedding Mass, which might lay him open to Protestant charges of 'idolatry'.

Mary's nobles were then invited to remove a pin each from her mourning robe, symbolically transforming her from widow to bride. For all her reservations about Darnley, she believed she had strengthened her position, and was determined to celebrate. Extensive festivities followed, over which Knox cast a jaundiced eye. 'During the space of three or four days,' he wrote tartly, 'there was nothing but balling, and dancing, and banquetting.'

The Protestant lords who had opposed the marriage – Moray, Châtelherault and Argyll – stayed away. Mary even went so far as to outlaw her brother Moray. They were already seeking Elizabeth's support in raising a rebellion.

1565 17 February	19 July	29 July	17 September	8 October
Mary and Darnley begin their courtship at Wemyss Castle in Fife.	**Mary recalls Bothwell** from exile.	**Mary marries** Henry Stewart, Lord Darnley.	**Bothwell disembarks** at Eyemouth, Berwickshire.	**On the last leg of the Chaseabout Raid,** Mary rides out against Moray, who retreats to England.

1565

1 September
Callendar House, near Falkirk
Playing chase

The travels of Mary and Darnley after their wedding have been characterised as a honeymoon – and it was around this time that their son James was conceived. But it would be a mistake to imagine this as a romantic sojourn. This was no time to relax: a rebellion was hatching.

When Darnley was proclaimed king on 30 July, the day after the wedding, the only voice raised in celebration was that of his father, the Earl of Lennox. The hostility towards Mary's new husband was palpable. In mid-August, there was a meeting of Protestant lords – among them Mary's half-brother Moray and the former regent, Châtelherault – in Ayr. They agreed to assemble an army by 24 August.

Meanwhile, on 19 August, Knox irked Darnley further by preaching in Edinburgh that, 'God justly punished Ahab and his posterity because he would not take order with that harlot Jezebel.'

Mary resolved to act swiftly and firmly. She had already begun the work of raising her own army, and put out a proclamation that the rebel lords were to meet her at Linlithgow on 24 August.

She and Darnley did not travel to Linlithgow until 26 August, riding at the head of an army of 8,000 to 10,000 men. This was the beginning of an extraordinary episode known as the Chaseabout Raid.

For several weeks, Mary's forces pursued those of the lords around the country, and a military encounter was expected almost daily.

Mary took relish in her role as military commander. She wore a pistol in her belt and a steel helmet on her head. Even Knox was impressed: 'Albeit the most part waxed weary, yet the queen's courage increased manlike so much that she was ever with the foremost,' he wrote. For his part, Darnley sported a gilt breastplate.

Finding no lords at Linlithgow, they proceeded west, towards where Moray had last been seen. Towards the end of August, Mary was at Glasgow and the lords' much smaller army passed through nearby Paisley, where they were within sight of the royal party.

The lords advanced to Edinburgh, entering via the West Port on 31 August, despite having the castle guns turned on them. However, they were unable to secure the city or drum up support, and withdrew to the south-west.

The following day, after heavy rain, the River Avon was in spate and Mary's forces were prevented from crossing. Unable to reach Edinburgh, she withdrew to Callendar House near Falkirk. This had been the hereditary residence of Alexander, 5th Lord Livingston, her former guardian, the father of Mary Livingston, one of the queen's 'Four Maries'.

It was here at Callendar House that the agreement had been signed in 1548, pledging Mary to marry the French dauphin. Her most recent visit had been just two months earlier, when she attended a Livingston baptism.

At Callendar, Mary changed tactics. Instead of heading south in direct pursuit of the lords, she turned north-east towards Fife. She had not finished with her half-brother yet.

1 Callendar House, childhood residence of Mary's companion Mary Livingston.

2 James Stewart, Earl of Moray, the most troublesome of Mary's many half-siblings.

16 September

Huntingtower Castle, Perthshire
Cat and mouse

Mary's main purpose in Fife was to cut off her brother's resources. Moray had been made secular prior of St Andrews at the age of seven, and his wealth derived mainly from this title.

Mary reached Dunfermline on 8 September, and stayed the night in the royal lodging attached to Dunfermline Abbey. It was here that, 35 years later, her grandson Charles I would be born – the last monarch born on Scottish soil.

From there she proceeded, via Lochleven and Falkland, to St Andrews, on the east coast of Fife, the cathedral seat from which Cardinal Beaton had led the pre-Reformation church. On 13 September, she issued a manifesto against the rebel lords from St Andrews.

She then proceeded via Dundee and Perth to Ruthven Castle (now known as Huntingtower) where she and Darnley spent the night of 16 September. This was the residence of Patrick, 3rd Lord Ruthven, a member of Mary's privy council and a supporter of Darnley, and they had stayed with him for two nights in June, a month before their wedding. But Ruthven was not a natural ally. In fact, it was said that Mary loathed him.

This probably related to his treatment of her mother, Mary of Guise. A staunch Protestant, he had been a member of the Lords of the Congregation who deposed her. Before that, during the Rough Wooing, he had negotiated secretly with the English, offering to surrender Perth in exchange for personal gain.

Before long, Ruthven would bring further trouble into Mary's life, but on this occasion he proved a serviceable host. The royal party made its way back to Edinburgh, where they arrived on 19 September.

The following day, a familiar figure appeared at Holyrood: the Earl of Bothwell, returned from exile in France. He had been effectively outlawed at the behest of Moray and Arran, but Mary had summoned him back. She now placed him in command of her forces against the rebels.

She also recruited the 5th Earl of Huntly, son of the rebellious earl who had died at the Battle of Corrichie. Both he and Bothwell detested Moray, and they became firm friends. Bothwell even married Huntly's sister, Jean Gordon, in February 1566.

On 8 October, wearing her steel helmet, flanked by Darnley and Bothwell, accompanied by an army of about 10,000 to 12,000 men, Mary rode towards Dumfries for a showdown with her brother.

No confrontation ever took place. Bereft of the support they had requested from Elizabeth I, the rebel lords knew they were beaten, and they melted away. Several, including Moray, fled to England.

Mary took Darnley to Lochmaben Castle, where her father had based himself before the disastrous Battle of Solway Moss. It was there that, on 14 October, they feasted and slept the sleep of the victorious.

3 Huntingtower Castle, known in Mary's time as Ruthven Castle.

4 A painted ceiling at Huntingtower, dating from Mary's era.

In the United Kingdom today, we have a constitutional monarchy – the Queen is the head of state, but legislation is passed by an elected parliament. While Royal Assent is required to make a bill into an Act of Parliament, this is a formality. The monarch is a ceremonial figurehead, required to be politically neutral, and remains unchanged despite changes in government. The Queen governs according to the constitution (unwritten in the United Kingdom), not according to her own will.

In Mary's day, the situation was very different.

The medieval and early modern monarch was expected to rule as well as reign. There were various means available to monarchs to enable them to rule effectively, with privy councils, general councils and parliament acting as bodies which could advise the monarch and carry out the royal will..

As the name suggests, the privy council was a relatively small group of advisors who were particularly close to the queen and in frequent contact with her. Its role was to offer advice on the day-to-day business of governing. It also had judicial functions, though these were increasingly transferred to the College of Justice (later the Court of Session, Scotland's supreme civil court) after its establishment in 1532.

The general council had a broader composition, consisting of earls, barons and members of the clergy. It had administrative, legislative and financial functions. The same was true of parliament, though this larger body also included representatives of the burghs (important for their financial contribution) and had greater powers than a general council. Specifically, it had a judicial function which the general council lacked.

By Mary's reign, the distinction between a full parliament and a general council was probably negligible. Bishops continued to sit in parliament, even after the Reformation, until 1638, when they were finally abolished.

Initially, either Catholic or Reformed bishops could sit but after 1567 Catholic bishops were excluded.

Parliament was not a permanent body, with a fixed location; and its members were not elected, but called up by the monarch. They were given 40 days' notice of sitting. Only four full parliaments were held during Mary's personal reign, supplemented by two conventions (essentially enlarged privy councils). All of these were held in Edinburgh, where parliament met in the central aisle of St Giles' Cathedral.

Attendance at parliament could vary considerably. In theory, all bishops, abbots, earls, barons, freeholders and representatives from the royal burghs attended, but not all those with the right to do so actually did. In reality, there were frequent problems getting enough attendees to carry out parliamentary business. Even at well-attended sessions, the number of members was considerably below modern levels. In 1558 for example, around 60 individuals were present, and sometimes there were even fewer sitters.

Parliament was not a rubber stamp for royal policy. It could and did criticise the monarch and act to limit royal plans. Its ability to do so, however, was dependent on the skill and power of the monarch and the prevailing political circumstances.

When Mary returned to Scotland she found that parliament had an increasing awareness of its role and power following the Reformation Parliament of 1560.

POLITICS AND POWER

This may explain the limited use of parliament during her reign, although her frequent travels did not suit the gathering of parliament. Nonetheless, legislation was passed, including Acts preventing the export of coal, an Act against witchcraft, sorcery and necromancy and one against the shooting of deer and other wild beasts with guns under pain of death.

Parliament was also a key forum for administering justice. While the privy council was also used for this, parliament was required for many types of judgement. It was for instance in parliament that the embalmed corpse of the Earl of Huntly was put on trial, and where the rebels of the Chaseabout Raid were forfeited.

Mary's position as dowager queen of France provided her with a substantial income, so she did not need regular general councils or parliaments to grant her taxation. Nonetheless parliament did grant taxation to meet some of the expenses for the baptismal celebrations of Prince James in 1566.

She made considerably more use of her privy council and, at least at first, the composition of this body was relatively balanced. It certainly included Catholic figures such as Huntly and anti-English individuals such as Bothwell. However, it also incorporated her half-brother James and other leaders of the Lords of the Congregation.

As a smaller body, the privy council was more mobile, and it could follow Mary on her frequent progresses around the country. By seeing and being seen, Mary was able to sustain the loyalty of many of her subjects. She had a talent for turning her visits into grand occasions, but was less effective in using her presence in the regions to learn about the political realities of her country. In one prominent example, Mary failed to suppress the beginnings of a feud in Argyll that would ultimately lead to the proscription of the clan MacGregor.

In France, Mary had been well taught how to reign. However, this proved a poor preparation for rule in Scotland, and she failed to manage the divergent personalities on her council.

A pre-Reformation dispute between the young Earl of Arran and Bothwell was rekindled within months of her return. As a result, Arran was confined as a madman and Bothwell fled the country.

In the early years of her personal reign, Mary sought to reassure her subjects by consulting her privy council regularly. Later, she began to seek advice from a limited number of household officers. Of itself, this was not a problem – monarchs often relied on a small core group of advisors. But it could cause resentment when traditional sources of advice were excluded in favour of foreign interlopers such as Rizzio or those of lower status. This helped bring about Rizzio's murder in 1566.

Another factor was Mary's decision to adopt a more pro-Catholic stance. Some Protestants began to fear for their religion and many Scots had concerns over the direction of foreign policy.

The use of favourites as political advisors could also cause problems when the monarch was as fickle as Mary appeared to be.

Far from nurturing long-term relationships with skilled and powerful nobles, the young queen had a tendency to acquire and discard favourites hastily, creating a dangerous instability. This continued even after Rizzio's death, although Mary did return to a more conciliatory and consultative form of government.

Mary's limited political skills became strikingly evident following the murder of Darnley. By failing to act as expected of a queen in mourning, and by showing such favouritism to the chief suspect, Bothwell, Mary once again demonstrated the limits of her knowledge and experience. In doing so, she alienated many of her subjects and potential supporters on the Continent.

Mary had charisma and courage, but was ineffective in managing her advisors, her privy council and her parliament with strength and consistency. This was, in the end, a core factor in her failure to rule effectively or successfully.

◀ The spire of St Giles' Cathedral in Edinburgh. The very few parliaments held during Mary's reign met in its central aisle.

1566

Conspiracy and Crisis

Mary had emerged triumphant from the Chaseabout Raid, her authority asserted; her enemies chastened; her marriage – for now – vindicated. By the start of 1566, she would also have been aware that she was pregnant. Delivery of the expected child would fulfil her duties as a monarch and as a wife, securing her succession – and promoting her dynastic claim to the English throne.

But this was to be an extremely turbulent year. The dissent she had so successfully suppressed would prove resurgent; her own private chambers would be violated in an unprecedented act of bloodshed; her marriage would grow increasingly shambolic; she would suffer her worst illness to date, barely escaping death; and the seeds would be planted for the central catastrophe of her reign – the murder of Darnley.

The year would also bring blessings, even if hindsight compels us to see the thorns beneath these roses. Her son and heir would arrive, fit and healthy, in June. He would be baptised in great splendour at a Catholic ceremony celebrated by Protestants – among them Queen Elizabeth of England.

And although Darnley proved a burdensome husband and royal consort, the intrepid Earl of Bothwell would emerge as a gallant and spirited companion, upon whose support Mary would come to rely ...

▶ The royal palace and great hall at Edinburgh Castle.

1566

Palace of Holyroodhouse, Edinburgh
Stabbing pains

David Rizzio is one of the best known figures in Mary's story, but he gained his fame in the worst way possible – as the victim of a savage murder.

Rizzio was a high-bred Catholic from Savoy, an independent duchy lying between France and Italy. He had come to Scotland with the Savoyard ambassador in 1561, initially finding favour with Darnley. He dressed flamboyantly and had a talent for music, both of which endeared him to the royal couple – indeed, Darnley was said to have taken him to bed.

In December 1564, Mary employed Rizzio as her personal secretary. This brought him into close contact with her and provoked considerable resentment among her retinue. In particular, it was a slight to her private secretary William Maitland of Lethington.

Meanwhile, relations between Mary and Darnley had declined. Their rows were becoming noisy and indiscreet. This was largely because Mary had failed to secure for Darnley the crown matrimonial, which would allow him to govern as king in his own right if she should die. Mary had an heir on the way, her popularity in England was growing, and she had the support of the new pope, Pius V. Her husband could almost be considered disposable.

Denied the crown matrimonial, Darnley began seeking recognition as a defender of the Catholic faith. He paraded his Catholic credentials, currying favour with Catholic potentates such as Philip II of Spain. He had even been plotting a counter-reformation – with Rizzio, among others.

But Darnley was both fickle and malleable. He was easily manipulated by Maitland, who was seeking the rehabilitation of Mary's brother, the Earl of Moray. Seeing this as a chance to overthrow Mary and become king in her place, Darnley took the simple step of changing his religion. He proposed to recall the exiled lords, and forbid any forfeit of their estates (a punishment due to be imposed by parliament). He soon enlisted the Earl of Morton and Lord Ruthven to this new conspiracy. It also gained Moray's approval.

What was needed was a scapegoat to account for Darnley's recent Catholic fervour.

Rizzio was coldly selected for this role. He was painted as a dangerous Catholic influence on the queen, encouraging her to propagate her faith and undermine the Reformation. It was even suggested that he was a secret agent of the Vatican. The rumour that he was having an affair with Mary – almost certainly spurious – certainly pricked Darnley's sense of jealousy, but his chief driver was ambition. Secret letters were exchanged with the English court, which clandestinely endorsed the plot.

Visitors to Holyrood Palace can still explore the precise spot where Rizzio was murdered, in Mary's private chambers in the north-west tower. They were dining together in her tiny supper room, with her sister Jean, Countess of Argyll.

The assassins were led by Lord Ruthven, who despite failing health saw fit to clad himself from head to foot in heavy armour.

1 A portrait of David Rizzio published in 1814, but said to be based on a portrait of 1564.

2 Rizzio's murder, as depicted by the 19th-century artist Sir William Allan.

1566

12 March
Dunbar Castle, East Lothian
Best served cold

Darnley led him via a secret passage to Mary's bedchamber, and sent a third man through Mary's suite to open the outer door to her presence chamber. This allowed about 80 rebels to enter the queen's private apartments from the main staircase.

When Ruthven appeared in the supper room, wheezily demanding 'yonder man Davie', both Mary and Rizzio knew there was serious cause for alarm. A brief parley followed, during which Mary cried treason. She was horrified to find her privacy violated and her authority overthrown – indeed she feared for her own life. One man – Andrew Ker of Fawdonside – even pointed a pistol directly at her.

Rizzio cowered behind Mary's skirts, but to no avail. She was manhandled into Darnley's arms and Rizzio was dragged through her bedchamber into the larger presence chamber. Surrounded by the rebels, he was stabbed more than 50 times. Darnley shrank from taking part, but one of the assassins grabbed his dagger and drove it into Rizzio's body, leaving it there as an emblem of Darnley's participation.

In the aftermath, the mob melted away and Ruthven returned to the supper room to confront Mary. She turned on Darnley, who countered that she had been denying him his conjugal rights, instead spending her evenings with Rizzio.

Eventually, Darnley and Ruthven departed, leaving Mary alone with an armed guard at her door. This had been an appalling ordeal for a reigning monarch – especially one who deplored violence. But worse was to come within a year.

After Rizzio's murder Mary found herself under house arrest and her reign – perhaps even her life – under threat. She knew she had to act quickly. She gained access to the four Maries, partly by pretending she was about to miscarry. Through them she requested support from Bothwell and Huntly.

The exiled lords of the Chaseabout Raid had returned to Edinburgh for the parliament of 12 March, at which they were due to be forfeited. Darnley had in fact cancelled the parliament, but Mary had devised a plan. She intended to pardon the lords while punishing Ruthven, Morton and Maitland for Rizzio's murder.

To appease Darnley and allay his suspicions of adultery, she offered to sleep with him at the end of the evening. He accepted ... but he was a heavy drinker, and it had been a long and stressful night. He failed to take up the offer.

The following morning, hungover but hopeful, he arrived in her bedchamber, but was rebuffed. Mary, by now six months pregnant, said she felt too ill for sex. Instead, she unveiled her new plan, for which she needed Darnley's co-operation. The lords would be told she was leaving Holyrood the following day, for the sake of her baby's health. They could propose their own terms for a pardon, which she would grant.

Having thus lulled the lords, Mary and Darnley stole from the palace at midnight via a secret passage. Horses were supplied by faithful servants and the couple rode to Dunbar, nearly 30 miles to the east. It was a five-hour journey, and Mary had to stop several times to be sick.

3 Darnley, who was manipulated by Mary into helping her escape Edinburgh after the murder of Rizzio.

But by early morning they were holed up at Dunbar Castle, a royal stronghold sited on a rocky promontory in the Firth of Forth.

By 18 March, Mary was ready to strike back. She returned to Edinburgh, where she would remain until the birth of her child. A fortnight later, from the safety of Edinburgh Castle, she outlawed Morton, Ruthven and all the other 80 participants in the Rizzio plot. Revenge was her reward for outsmarting her husband and those who had rebelled against her, and we can be sure it tasted sweet.

Later Visit
Mary was to return to Dunbar just over a year later. By that time, both she and the castle had fallen into Bothwell's hands. (See page 92.)

19 June

Edinburgh Castle
Mary's boy child

Mary forewent the comforts of Holyrood when the time came to give birth. She lodged instead in the palace block at Edinburgh Castle, which was less commodious but more secure. This must have seemed a priority after Rizzio's murder.

She took to her confinement on 3 June, and soon afterwards set to work on her will. Even for a queen, childbirth was a dangerous business, and her country was turbulent enough without a monarch dying intestate.

She set out plans for the country to be jointly ruled by a triumvirate, which included the Earl of Argyll and John, Lord Erskine, whom she made Earl of Mar. The third party may or may not have been Darnley. Three copies were made of the will, but all have been lost.

The beneficiaries numbered fewer than 60, a quarter of whom were her Guise relatives. The four Maries were to receive modest bequests, as was Darnley. Her other worldly goods were to be distributed among Scottish friends and relations.

She went into labour on 19 June, and by all accounts it was a long and painful process. In the absence of gas and air, Margaret, Countess of Atholl, took it upon herself to try witchcraft.

She transferred Mary's pains onto the nominated wet-nurse, Margaret, Lady Reres, whose resulting agonies did not seem to alleviate Mary's at all.

James was born between 10am and 11am, and was immediately seen to be very robust and lively. A 'caul' – a remnant of the amniotic sac – covered his face, which was thought to signify an immunity from death by drowning. The appearance of a healthy, legitimate male heir was a triumph for Mary, and prompted wild jubilation among Catholics and Protestants alike. The castle's guns boomed in salute and 500 bonfires blazed on the hills around Edinburgh.

On 24 June, the new prince was presented to Henry Killigrew, the new English ambassador, who described him as, 'all to my judgement well proportioned and like to prove a goodly prince,' recalling the words of his predecessor Sir Ralph Sadler, speaking about the infant Mary.

The news was carried to Elizabeth I by one of Mary's most faithful courtiers, Sir James Melville. She is said to have responded, 'Alack, the queen of Scots is lighter of a bonny son, and I am but of barren stock.'

James's birth changed everything. Within a year, he would be king, his father dead and his mother imprisoned.

1566 7 January	9 March	19 June	October	17 December	24 December
Pope Pius V succeeds Pope Pius IV as pope.	**David Rizzio** murdered in Mary's private apartment at Holyrood.	At Edinburgh Castle, **Mary gives birth** to a son, the future King James VI of Scotland and I of England.	**Mary suffers a life-threatening illness** at Jedburgh.	**Baptism of Prince James** at Stirling.	**Mary pardons** Rizzio's murderers.

1566

29 July
Alloa Tower, Clackmannanshire
Trouble and strife

After a period of recuperation from childbirth, Mary needed a break. She decided to take a short holiday in central Scotland.

It was high summer, and she left Edinburgh with her reconciled half-brother Moray and her trusted retainer Bothwell. They departed by boat from Newhaven, travelling up the River Forth to Alloa. They were guests there of John Erskine, the new Earl of Mar, at his grand tower house.

Also present was the French ambassador Michel de Castelnau, who – on the orders of Catherine de' Medici, queen dowager of France – had the thankless task of attempting to reconcile Mary to Darnley.

Darnley did turn up, briefly, at Alloa. It was the anniversary of their wedding, but by now their relationship had broken down almost completely. Mary refused to eat or sleep with him, and upbraided him in terms which the English ambassador, the Earl of Bedford, wrote, 'cannot for modesty … be reported'.

For his part, Darnley was obsessively jealous, given to heavy drinking, 'vagabondizing' and violent rages. He departed after a few hours and was not seen for several days. He had other matters to distract him, such as hatching a woefully misguided plot for an invasion of the British Isles by European Catholic powers. It came to nothing.

1566

19 August
Traquair House, near Peebles
Further trouble and strife

By mid-August Mary must have recovered her health, for she spent two or three days hunting near Selkirk in the Borders. From there, she visited Traquair House, before heading north for another hunting trip in Perthshire.

Traquair is said to be the oldest continuously occupied residence in Scotland, visited by 27 monarchs. A royal hunting lodge has existed on this site since the 1100s, though most of the present building is later. Mary's host was Sir John Stewart, 4th Laird of Traquair, Captain of the Queen's Bodyguard.

The room where Mary probably slept is on the first floor of the original 12th-century tower. It still holds a bed and a cradle both dating from the 1500s. The bed was used by Mary at Terregles Castle, a Maxwell seat near Dumfries, and came here in the 1890s.

The cradle, however, is believed to have been slept in by the infant James at Traquair.

Darnley accompanied Mary on this visit. She claimed that she was paving the way for reconciliation, but it was not a happy evening. Mary announced that she was pregnant again and withdrew from the hunt. Darnley responded with conspicuous tactlessness, saying: 'If we lose this one, we will make another.'

The gallant Sir John reportedly scolded the young king for his bad manners. Darnley's riposte was, 'What! Ought we not to work a mare when she is in foal?'

He evidently believed Mary was pregnant, which suggests he must have gained access to her bed. But if the queen was indeed 'in foal' there would be no offspring to show for it.

3 The bedchamber where Mary and the infant Prince James are thought to have slept at Traquair House.

1566

15 October

Hermitage Castle, Borders
A mercy dash

Few of Mary's exploits lend themselves better to romantic fiction than her long and perilous journey to visit the wounded Bothwell. This episode has often been characterised as a lovers' tryst: the reality is perhaps even more dramatic.

Mary was on her way to Jedburgh in the Borders when news reached her that Bothwell had been ambushed and killed. His assailants were the Elliots of Liddesdale, a notorious family of reivers, or border cattle thieves. As lieutenant of the Borders, Bothwell had the task of policing a notoriously lawless region and had incurred the Elliots' hatred.

But Bothwell was not dead after all; just badly wounded. He had been carried on a cart to Hermitage Castle, one of Scotland's most daunting medieval strongholds, a Bothwell property since the 1490s.

Bandaged and bleeding, the earl lay groaning in his quarters. These were probably in the Douglas Tower, the largest and grandest of the castle's four corner towers, built for William, 1st Earl of Douglas, a former lord of Liddesdale.

Mary had barely left Edinburgh when she received the news, but she had business to attend to. She was to attend a justice ayre, or local court hearing, in Jedburgh – and she did so as planned. It was not until a week later, when the court had completed its session, that she left to visit her trusted earl.

That said, the trip had an air of urgency about it. Mary rode virtually non-stop all the way to Hermitage, a journey of about 25 miles, across rough terrain. Those who later sought to besmirch her reputation were at pains to portray her haste as romantic ardour, but there is no solid evidence to support an affair with Bothwell at this stage.

In fact, Mary travelled to Hermitage accompanied by her brother Moray and several other nobles. (Darnley was absent, having argued with her yet again over his royal status, and was now threatening to emigrate.) She remained with Bothwell at Hermitage only two hours, then returned to Jedburgh, where the justice ayre was to reconvene the following day. Bothwell had been planning to attend it himself, and one purpose of Mary's visit may have been a briefing. But she must certainly have been concerned for the wellbeing of one of her staunchest allies.

It was a long, arduous journey, even by the standards of the time, when it was not uncommon to travel 50 miles on horseback in a single day. According to legend, Mary was thrown from her horse in a boggy area near Hermitage now known as Queen's Mire – and a watch thought to belong to her was indeed found there. In any event, the trip seems to have brought on another bout of illness – and this was to be the worst of Mary's entire life.

1 The watch recovered from the Queen's Mire, near Hermitage Castle, where Mary is said to have lost her watch.

2 Hermitage Castle's imposing east facade.

3 The castle in its isolated position, dominating Liddesdale.

15 October–9 November

Mary Queen of Scots' House, Jedburgh
A scrape with death

On her return to Jedburgh from Hermitage, Mary suffered what could easily have been a fatal collapse. It was the worst health crisis in a life dogged by illness, and it left the throne in a vulnerable position.

Mary had rarely enjoyed the best of health. In the harrowing weeks after her round trip to Hermitage, she came close to death. She complained of sharp abdominal pain, suffered convulsions, repeatedly lost consciousness, vomited blood, lost her sight and hearing and became stiff and cold – indeed, at one point she was thought to have died.

The most likely cause of her symptoms was a ruptured gastric ulcer, though there may have been other causes too. She had undergone a troubled labour just four months earlier, and her marriage to Darnley was a source of considerable stress. Mary's wayward husband was widely held responsible, and none of the privy councillors had any appetite for his claim on the throne should she die.

Our uncertainty as to the nature of her illness reflects the limited medical knowledge of the time. Fortunately, Mary's French physician, Charles Nau, was on hand: he almost certainly saved her life. The therapy – which today reads like a crank cure – included tight bandaging of the arms, legs and big toes. Vomiting and diarrhoea were induced by a combination of wine administered orally and an enema, purging the patient of a large quantity of 'corrupt' blood.

A few hours later, she began to recover, though her convalescence took well over a week.

The fortified 'bastel house' where Mary is thought to have stayed throughout her illness belonged to her loyal supporter, Sir Thomas Kerr of Ferniehirst. (He was the son-in-law of Sir William Kirkcaldy of Grange, governor of Edinburgh Castle, and both men would distinguish themselves defending the castle in Mary's name during the Lang Siege of 1571–3.) Records show that she was entertained during her stay by a lutenist called John Hume and a whistle-player called James Heron. She paid rent of £40 Scots.

The house still stands on Queen Street, not far from Jedburgh Abbey. It now houses a Mary Queen of Scots visitor centre, where the watch found in the Queen's Mire is displayed. In common with other Kerr residences, it features a left-handed spiral staircase, supposedly to impart an advantage to a left-handed swordsman.

Darnley did pay his ailing wife a brief overnight visit, before once more taking umbrage and departing to his family seat in Glasgow. It was the gallant Bothwell, himself still recuperating from his injuries, who attended a meeting of the privy council in Jedburgh. Afterwards, in his capacity as lieutenant of the Borders, he accompanied Mary's party for a brief and uneventful progress through Berwickshire and East Lothian.

4 A 16th-century woodcut of a lutenist. Mary was entertained by musicians during her convalescence at Jedburgh.

5 The house owned by Sir Thomas Kerr of Ferniehirst, where Mary is thought to have stayed during her illness.

1566

Tantallon Castle, East Lothian
Redbeard's castle

Even as a ruin, Tantallon Castle is a majestic sight, a mighty crescent of red sandstone on a clifftop at the mouth of the Firth of Forth. It is defended on its landward side by two deep ditches and a ravelin – a raised barrier built from earth. And as its strategic position and its defences suggest, it has had a colourful history.

Tantallon had long been a castle of the Douglases, for centuries one of Scotland's most powerful families. According to the 16th-century chronicler Robert Lindsay of Pitscottie, 'There durst none strive with a Douglas, nor yet with a Douglas's man; for if he did, he was sure to get the worse.'

Built around 1350 by William, 1st Earl of Douglas, Tantallon passed in 1389 to the junior branch of the family – the 'Red Douglases'. It remained in their hands for nearly two centuries, surviving sieges by both James IV in 1491 and James V in 1528. (The second of these was an act of revenge. Archibald Douglas, 6th Earl of Angus, had married James IV's widow, Margaret Tudor, and had held her son James V captive at Edinburgh Castle. But the siege failed, largely due to shortage of ammunition.)

It was not until 1529 that James V laid claim to his former stepfather's castle, while Angus was exiled in England.

He had its defences improved, using green basalt, which gave the castle its piebald appearance. Angus regained the castle in 1543, and used it to aid the English during the Rough Wooing. Mary of Guise seized it after his death in 1557.

By 1565, following several more changes of custody, Tantallon was in the hands of James Douglas, Earl of Morton, one of the most powerful – and perfidious – of Mary's Protestant lords. By now it was owned by the Crown and Morton was required to keep it 'reddie and patent to Her Majestie'.

He was relieved of this task before her visit. As one of the many conspirators in the Rizzio murder plot, Morton was disgraced, and one of his key penalties was losing Tantallon, which was now occupied by Robert Lauder of Bass.

A few months passed before Mary's first and only visit to the castle, on the homeward leg of her brief progress in the south-east, after her life-threatening illness at Jedburgh.

For now, Morton had been neutralised, but he would be back, eventually governing Scotland as regent. Before that, he would make further trouble for the queen.

1 A stone cannonball dating from the 1400s or 1500s, found below the cliffs near the castle.

2 James Douglas, 4th Earl of Morton, disgraced for his role in the plot against Rizzio.

3 The striking ruins of Tantallon Castle.

1566

20 November–7 December

Craigmillar Castle, near Edinburgh
The plot thickens

In November, Mary sought sanctuary with a favoured ally to recuperate from the debilitating events of the past few months. It was during this time that the most damaging conspiracy of her reign began to take root.

From Tantallon, Mary travelled west to Craigmillar Castle, a couple of miles south of Edinburgh. This imposing medieval stronghold – today an extensive and picturesque ruin – was the main residence of Sir Simon Preston. He was one of her most loyal supporters, and she had appointed him both as a privy councillor and as Provost of Edinburgh.

The other members of her privy council were also present – they included her half-brother Moray, Huntly, Argyll, Maitland and Bothwell.

She had been to Craigmillar before, in September 1563, but this visit of more than a fortnight was her longest. Her French retinue lodged nearby, in an area known to this day as Little France.

At Craigmillar her illness returned and she sank into a morbid mood. 'I could wish to be dead,' she was reportedly heard to say. She had clearly been contemplating mortality, for she had been in negotiation with Elizabeth I, to whom she wished to entrust the care of her son, in the event of her own death.

As she recovered, she was largely left alone by her husband, whose occasional visits generally led to arguments. With Darnley out of the way, the lords began scheming about how to get rid of him. A divorce – or at least a separation – would weaken him, but they feared his father, the Earl of Lennox, might be powerful enough to stage a coup.

Besides, the lords, and particularly Maitland, wanted to see Darnley brought low; they also hoped to gain a pardon for Morton and the other conspirators in Rizzio's murder.

Mary, still in her sickbed, agreed in principle to a dissolution of the marriage, provided her son's legitimacy and her own honour were not harmed.

According to tradition, a 'Craigmillar Bond' was drawn up during this period, in which the lords pledged themselves to Darnley's murder. However, the original document has never been found, and it may well have been invented during the cover-ups that would follow.

The decision to murder Darnley was probably not reached for another few weeks, but the net was closing in on him.

4 Craigmillar Castle, where Mary's councillors plotted against Darnley.

5 Mary's secretary of state, Sir William Maitland of Lethington.

6 The arms of Sir Simon Preston, which can still be seen at Craigmillar.

17 December

Stirling Castle
The absentee father

In the later stages of her pregnancy, with Rizzio's murder fresh in her mind, Mary had taken to Edinburgh Castle for security. Now, after the birth of her son, she transferred him to Stirling Castle – perhaps an even safer lodging for a child whose kidnap would undermine her completely. But when the time came to baptise the infant prince, there was another reason to choose Stirling: it was now the only chapel royal in Scotland suitable for a major Catholic ceremony.

James's birth was a triumph for Mary, settling her succession, and she was determined to stage a glorious, unprecedented spectacle to mark its significance. The celebrations were modelled on royal fêtes she had attended in France, and lasted three days. All the major European diplomats were invited. The cost was well beyond Mary's pocket, but parliament granted her a taxation of £12,000 to cover the money she borrowed from Edinburgh merchants to pay for it.

The religious ceremony was carried out by John Hamilton, Archbishop of St Andrews. The illegitimate brother of the former Regent Arran (now Duke of Châtelherault), Hamilton had succeeded the murdered Cardinal Beaton in 1546 as head of the pre-Reformation Church.

The prince was carried into the chapel by the Count of Brienne, acting as proxy for King Charles XI of France, younger brother of Mary's late husband Francis II. Traditionally, the priest officiating at a baptism would spit into the child's mouth; however Mary forbade this. It has been suggested that Hamilton suffered from syphilis.

1 James aged about five, in a portrait by the court painter Arnold Bronckhorst.

2 An artist's impression of the 'enchanted fortress' erected for the occasion just outside Stirling Castle.

The font used for the ceremony was a magnificent gift from Elizabeth I, whom Mary had flatteringly appointed as James's godmother. Cast in gold and encrusted with gemstones, it was said to weigh at least 28lb (12.7kg). This was a conspicuous bestowal of approval from England, and coincided with fresh negotiations over the succession, under which Mary was to be named as heir apparent to the English throne.

Elizabeth stopped short of attending in person, but she was represented by Mary's half-sister Jean, Countess of Argyll. She may have been the only Protestant attending the ceremony. The English ambassador, the Earl of Bedford, was one of a number of Protestants who waited outside the chapel. The countess was later scolded by John Knox for this unseemly brush with Catholicism, but it seems she conducted herself with great dignity.

Among the event's many extravagances were fancy new outfits Mary had ordered for her retinue. Her half-brother Moray was clad in green, Argyll in red and Bothwell in blue. There were also outfits of cloth of silver and cloth of gold, and it was said that everyone was dressed well above their rank.

Among the entertainments were masques (highly stylised dramatic performances) written by the scholar George Buchanan and staged by Mary's favoured valet Bastian Pagès. Their theme was reconciliation, and they were intended to hint that Mary was contemplating a pardon for Rizzio's killers.

There was also a pasteboard enchanted fortress erected in the Valley – the dip between castle and town. The guests watched from a specially built viewing platform as it was besieged by a marauding band of allegorical figures including Moors, centaurs and fiends. To mark the end of the festivity, the sky was lit up by fireworks, gunpowder and cannon fire.

Before that, though, came the final and grandest banquet. Food was served from a mechanical moving stage, operated by satyrs and nymphs. An angel appeared from the ceiling in a golden sphere, reciting verses. There was an angry response when Pagès' satyrs waggled their posteriors at the English party, but aside from that the whole event went smoothly until the stage collapsed, just as the final course was served.

There was, however, a notable absentee. Darnley was nowhere to be seen, though he was known to be skulking somewhere in the castle. He was still furious at being denied the crown matrimonial that would secure his status as king. Several commentators remarked on this flagrant failure of etiquette.

By contrast, Bothwell enjoyed a very prominent role in the proceedings. He it was, in his lavish blue suit, who greeted the ambassadors and stood behind Mary's chair at the final banquet, though he was among the Protestants who had declined to attend the baptismal service. He had even been reconciled – nominally – with his old foes, Moray and Argyll.

It was about this time, with Bothwell so clearly in favour, that rumours began to circulate about the nature of his relationship with the queen. They were probably unfounded, but in due course they would prove very useful to her enemies.

3 Elizabeth I of England, who was appointed as James's godmother. She did not attend the baptism but sent a solid gold font as a gift.

Mary was born into a nation in the early stages of a medical revolution. It would be nearly 300 years before Scotland led the field in medical expertise, but the seeds had been planted.

1 The medicinal herb feverfew, still used in traditional remedies today.

2 The Flemish anatomist Andreas Vesalius, author of a highly influential textbook of 1543.

A key instigator was Mary's grandfather, James IV, an enthusiastic patron of science and medicine. King's College, Aberdeen, founded during his reign, employed a mediciner – a teacher of medicine – from its inception.

Another crucial development was the Incorporation of Surgeons and Barbers of Edinburgh, whose charter James IV ratified in 1506. Founded to pursue knowledge and exclude practitioners who lacked it, this body began the trend towards professional, and secular, medicine. Prior to this, medical knowledge – like most learning – had resided in the monasteries.

Despite the growth of medical knowledge in the 1500s, it was not possible to study and graduate as a physician in Scotland. (At this time, a physician was considered superior to a surgeon, in both intellect and status.) Any Scot seeking to practise physic would travel to the Continent to study. Famous medical schools had been founded at cities including Paris, Padua, Reims and Amiens. It is not surprising that Mary chose to bring French physicians such as Charles Nau back with her to Scotland.

A key medical textbook of the day was *De Humani Corporis Fabrica* ('On the Structure of the Human Body') (1543) by Andreas Vesalius, a professor at Padua who is considered the founder of modern anatomy. Another leading medical writer of the time was the French surgeon Ambroise Paré. He had treated battlefield injuries, and he vividly describes the challenges faced by medicine after the emergence of artillery and other firearms.

Mary herself recognised the importance of medics on the battlefield. In 1567 she declared surgeons exempt from bearing arms in battle – with the philanthropic proviso that they must treat the wounded of *both* sides.

The rapid growth of printing technologies led to a great propagation of information. The first medical text to be published in Scots is thought to be *Ane Breve Description of the Pest*, which appeared soon after Mary's abdication in 1568, during an outbreak of bubonic plague. The author was Gilbert Skeyne, then holding the mediciner's post at Aberdeen.

Skeyne accurately identified environmental factors for the spread of disease: stagnant water, mud, dung, 'stinkand cloisettis' (stinking latrines) and 'deid cariounis vnbureit' (unburied rotting flesh), but concluded that 'the principal preservative cure of the pest is to returne to God'.

This reminds us that understanding of the body, its functions and its pathology were quite different from modern medical science. The chief influences on Renaissance medicine were still the great Classical pioneers, Hippocrates and Galen, together with ideas drawn from Arabic medicine.

Orthodox medical theory centred on the four humours and their associated temperaments: blood (sanguine); black bile (melancholic); yellow bile (choleric); and phlegm (phlegmatic). Imbalances were thought to cause most ailments, and if this seems bizarre we should also bear in mind that a sound knowledge of astrological signs was considered a proper part of medical study, and comets were often cited as a cause of human illness.

SICKNESS AND HEALTH

Ill-health was treated in a number of ways, a chief one being bloodletting – a treatment Mary received on numerous occasions. The ancient practice of trepanning – boring a hole in the skull – was still widely used. Urine was closely inspected for signs of illness. Purging and enemas were common, and treatment using charmstones was by no means unusual. Wounds were often cauterised with hot pitch.

The medicines prescribed by trained physicians included many of the same ingredients as folk remedies. They included juniper, rhubarb, myrrh, mint, oregano, rosewater, vinegar and the evocatively named herb, feverfew. One treatment for convulsions was prepared in a particularly nasty way, by roasting a live mole, then pulverising it with crushed amber.

Epidemics were common in the 1500s, and not limited to bubonic plague. Syphilis, originally known as grandgore, had only been identified in the 1490s. It may have been brought to the British Isles in 1495 by mercenaries hired by Perkin Warbeck, pretender to the English throne. A major epidemic hit Scotland in 1497, when it was described in Aberdeen's Town Council Minutes as 'the infirmity cumm out of Franche'.

Leprosy was also at large, and town councils took precautions to segregate sufferers. An edict regarding the accommodation of lepers was issued in Edinburgh in 1567.

In general, good health depended more on luck than on medical science. Queen Mary had access to the best physicians of the day, yet she suffered atrocious health – though it was Nau's intervention that saved her life at Jedburgh in 1566.

Her many bouts of illness were characterised by abdominal pain, vomiting, swooning and listlessness. Her symptoms often lasted several days or even weeks, after which she typically made a sudden recovery and returned to the healthy outdoor pursuits she so enjoyed.

During her life, her illness was generally attributed to black bile, though her adolescent bout of smallpox was correctly diagnosed and treated, her pustules lanced without scarring.

At 13, she suffered a recurrent fever known as 'quartan ague'. A burst gastric ulcer seems the most likely cause of her near-fatal illness at Jedburgh.

Stress was almost certainly a major factor in Mary's health, and she tended to fall ill when she was under personal pressure. Her diet was anything but meagre, but with such an abundance of food on offer, she must have yielded to the temptation to overeat, and in later life, with little opportunity to exercise, she gained weight and developed digestive problems.

Her imprisonment in England could not be described as harsh, but some of it was spent in damp conditions, which brought on her rheumatism. By the time of her death, she was in a bad way, with swollen, ulcerated legs, an inflamed heel, a stiff arm and an open sore on her shoulder. In the light of this, her words on receiving news of her execution have a ring of truth: 'You will do me a great good in withdrawing me from this world.'

2

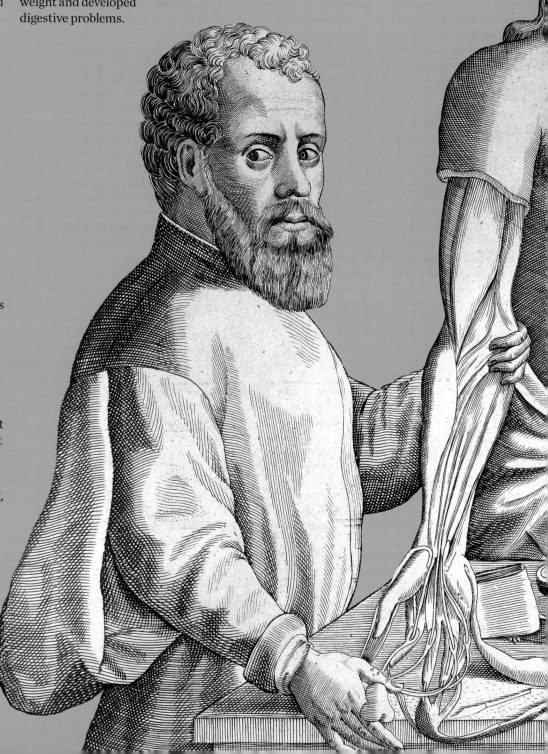

1567-8

Murder, Mayhem and Misery

Something was going to have to be done about Darnley. The queen's husband had become a problem for everyone around him.

On the one hand he was conniving and ruthlessly ambitious, continually scheming to gain the crown for himself, with little regard for Mary's status or wellbeing. When left unsupervised, he would busy himself with plots and conspiracies – one reason why his threat to emigrate was so alarming.

On the other hand, he was entirely inadequate for the royal role he coveted: dissolute, irresponsible, moody, vain and attention-seeking.

On top of all that, he had contracted syphilis, though he does not appear to have passed it to Mary. In the winter of 1566–7, the disease moved into its secondary phase, bringing him out in a purulent skin rash and disfiguring his youthful good looks.

Even Mary, who clung to the appearance of decorum, acknowledged that her marriage had failed. 'He misuses himself so far towards her that it is an heartbreak for her to think that he should be her husband,' Maitland wrote to Archbishop Beaton, the Scottish ambassador in France.

The crucial question was this: what steps was Mary prepared to take to be rid of her husband? He was the father of the heir apparent, and nominally the king. He could not simply be divorced or sidelined and allowed to return to his schemes.

Some of Mary's lords were not long in deciding what must be done. But their solution would bring disaster for her. From that point forward, the greatest enigma overhanging her reign, and the long period of imprisonment that followed, was whether she had condoned their actions or not.

▶ The view from the chamber where Mary spent most of her time at Lochleven Castle.

1567

21 January
Place of Stablegreen, Glasgow
The English patient

1 A portrait thought to depict Darnley's father, Matthew Stewart, 4th Earl of Lennox, who later governed Scotland as Regent Lennox.

10 February
Kirk o' Field, Edinburgh
Boom time

In mid-January, a secret meeting took place at Whittinghame Tower in East Lothian. Those attending included Bothwell, Maitland and the newly returned Morton. He had been pardoned at Christmas for Rizzio's murder and was now seeking vengeance against the double-crossing Darnley. The outcome of the meeting was a murder plot.

The intended victim was of course Darnley, who had meanwhile heard rumours of a plan to kidnap him. Fleeing Stirling, he sought refuge at the Glasgow residence of his father, the Earl of Lennox. The house was close to Glasgow Cathedral, on a site now occupied by Barony North Church. On his way there, Darnley became sick with the onset of secondary syphilis.

Mary was at Holyrood, pursuing her delicate negotiations over the English succession. Then she learned from an informer that Darnley was plotting to kidnap Prince James, stage a coronation and govern as regent, keeping Mary prisoner. It was another unworkable fantasy, but alarming enough to spur her to action. She decided to coax Darnley back to Edinburgh and keep him out of trouble at Craigmillar. She set off for Glasgow on 20 January.

The husband she found there the next day was not the handsome youth she had married. The disease had brought him out in foul-smelling pustules all over his body. His treatment involved bathing in sulphur and drinking mercury, which was rotting his gums and loosening his teeth.

He looked and smelled repulsive, but Mary knew how to win him round. She promised to restore marital relations once he had recovered.

During Mary's stay in Glasgow, it was later claimed, she wrote two incriminating letters to Bothwell. These were the most significant of the documents that came to be known as the Casket Letters (see page 104.)

Darnley eventually consented to return to Edinburgh, but refused to go to Craigmillar, since he hated its owner Sir Simon Preston. Nor did he wish to be seen at Holyrood in his disfigured state. Instead, he took up residence on the outskirts of the city at Kirk o' Field.

Kirk o' Field is an essential location in this story. In a sense, Mary's whole life pivoted on the incident that occurred here. Yet nothing at all remains of the building.

The house was part of the Black Friars' monastery, founded by Alexander II in 1230. As its name implies, Kirk o' Field originally lay outside Edinburgh, though the city wall had been extended in the 1500s. Darnley was housed in the Old Provost's Lodging, at the precinct's southern side, close to a postern – a rear door in the city wall. It now lies under the pavement at the corner of South Bridge and South College Street.

Part of the reason Kirk o' Field has vanished is that it was largely destroyed on the night in question. Like the conspiracy of 1605, intended to assassinate Darnley's son, James VI and I, this was a gunpowder plot.

In an account of 1568, specifically designed to incriminate Mary, George Buchanan declared the Old Provost's Lodging unfitting accommodation: 'a house not commodious for a sick man, nor comely for a king, for it was both ruined and ruinous, and has stood empty without any dweller in it for divers years'.

This was largely fiction: the house was in sound condition and had been made pretty comfortable. Darnley's chamber was on the upper floor, decorated with six expensive tapestries confiscated from the Huntly earls after the Battle of Corrichie. There was also a small Turkish carpet and a high chair upholstered in purple velvet.

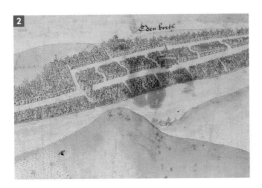

2 Edinburgh as depicted
by an English spy in
1544. The church top
centre of this detail is
Kirk o' Field.

3 The scene of Darnley's
murder, in an illustration
copied from the one
sent to Cecil.

His bed, swathed in violet velvet and embellished with cloth of silver and gold, had originally belonged to Mary of Guise (it is the model for the replica bed now displayed at Stirling Palace). It had been given to him by his wife, and an inferior bed had been removed to make space for it. He also had a bathtub in his chamber, for his treatments.

Mary also slept at Kirk o'Field for a couple of nights, in the room below Darnley's. She was convivial, playing cards with him until late into the night. On the night of 9 February, however, she was at Holyrood Palace, celebrating the marriage of her valet and stage designer Bastian Pagès. This allowed the conspirators to smuggle a huge quantity of explosives into her bedchamber.

At just after 2am on 10 February, a terrific explosion ripped through the house, reducing it to rubble. Anyone inside the house would have been killed for certain. The Register of the Privy Council records that, 'The house … was in an instant blown in the air … with such a force and vehemency that of the whole lodging walls and other there is no thing left unruinated … to the very ground stone.'

But Darnley, mysteriously, was not inside. His body, unmarked by the explosion, was soon found in a nearby garden, alongside that of his bedchamber servant William Taylor. They had been suffocated or strangled.

A group of women living nearby gave evidence (though it was suppressed) that they had seen a group of well-dressed men lurking in the alley outside the house. Darnley's voice had been heard pleading for mercy from 'my kinsmen' (these would have been the Douglas party, related to his mother).

The most likely explanation is that a slow fuse was lit and Darnley, having heard a noise and sensed danger, escaped the house. Taylor may have helped him, lowering him from the window in a chair. But they had been seized by the mob and strangled, their corpses dumped before the explosives went off.

There would be many subsequent attempts to implicate Mary in the murder, but the evidence is weak at best. The use of her bedchamber played into the hands of her accusers, and it was Mary who had persuaded Darnley to return to Edinburgh – but this was more likely to keep him under surveillance than to lure him to his death.

Of the main conspirators, only Morton was ever convicted, and not until years later. The rumour mill was not slow to identify Bothwell as the chief suspect, and flyers accusing him of the king's murder soon began to appear around town. On this occasion, he refrained from challenging anyone to a duel, keeping a relatively low profile.

As for Mary, if she was involved, she made a good show of being horrified by the incident. She offered a reward of £2,000 and even a pardon to anyone turning queen's evidence. However, she delayed placing the court in mourning and gave little outward sign of grief. She even gave some of Darnley's clothes to Bothwell, who was widely considered the obvious culprit. Suspicion soon fell on her, not only at home but from her French relations and from England.

Elizabeth wrote to her: 'I will not conceal from you that people for the most part are saying that you will look through your fingers at this deed instead of avenging it … I beg you … that you will not fear to touch even him whom you have nearest to you if he was involved.' Negotiations over the English succession ground to a halt.

1567

23 April

Stirling Castle
Sweet sorrow

Events moved very quickly in the months following Darnley's murder. He was buried without ceremony on 14 February, and although Mary collapsed at a requiem Mass on 23 March, there was a general perception that her mourning was none too sincere. For example, it took her fully five days to order the traditional black taffeta to drape around her lodgings.

Afraid for her own life, she placed her faith in Bothwell. Although he was clearly a murder suspect, she had obviously decided he could be trusted. She had, after all, been betrayed at some point by most of her senior lords, and Bothwell commanded her bodyguard, so she felt safest with him.

They were frequently seen together. For example, on 26 February, they competed at archery against Huntly and Argyll – and won. Mary left Prince James in Bothwell's care when she visited Seton Palace, the residence of her master of the household, Lord Seton, 10 miles east of Edinburgh. Later, Bothwell accompanied her to Seton.

Whether Mary suspected it or not, Bothwell had ulterior motives, and the rumour mill had noticed. At Easter, they found themselves the subject of scurrilous and highly insulting gossip.

Placards began to appear around Edinburgh depicting a mermaid and a hare. The mermaid was topless, crowned and flanked by the initials 'MR' – Maria Regina. The hare, encircled by swords, was labelled 'IH' – James Hepburn – i.e. Bothwell, whose family emblem was a hare. The image was laced with erotic symbolism that would not have been lost on educated people of the day. The core message was to link Mary sexually with Bothwell, and both with the murder. It was a deep affront to her dignity and authority.

On 10 April, Bothwell stood trial for Darnley's murder at the Tolbooth in Edinburgh. He arrived at the head of 4,000 men, showing his usual swagger. His confidence was well placed. He was acquitted, and immediately posted a placard at the Tolbooth, declaring his innocence and issuing his customary challenge to a duel. No one took up the gauntlet.

At a sitting of parliament on 16 April, Morton, Argyll and Huntly had their lands restored, while Bothwell was granted Dunbar Castle. Three days later, with the parliament completed, Bothwell invited his fellow senior lords to dinner at Ainslie's Tavern in Edinburgh.

He had prepared a document he wanted them to sign: a declaration that he was their approved choice as the queen's new husband. Only Huntly and Morton were persuaded to sign, and this was not quite good enough for Bothwell. He decided to act quickly and decisively.

On 21 April, Mary went on horseback to Stirling Castle, where her son had spent the past month in the care of the Earl of Mar. She intended to bring him to Edinburgh, but Mar refused to release the child, fearing the consequences if he fell into Bothwell's hands. Mary was furious, but Mar stood his ground.

After two nights, Mary left the castle without her ten-month-old son. She cannot have known that she would never see him again.

1 Stirling Castle, where Mary saw her son for the last time.

2 John Erskine, Earl of Mar, custodian of the young prince.

1567 9 February	15 May	15 June	17 June	24 July	29 July
Darnley's assassination at Kirk o'Field, Edinburgh.	**Mary marries** James Hepburn, 4th Earl of Bothwell.	**Mary surrenders** to her nobles at Carberry Hill, near Musselburgh.	**Mary is imprisoned** at Lochleven Castle.	**Mary is forced to abdicate** in favour of her one-year-old son James VI.	**James VI is crowned** at Stirling. The sermon is preached by John Knox.

3 The 'mermaid and hare' placard which linked Mary sexually with Bothwell, and Bothwell with Darnley's murder.

Spot the odd one out

This well known painting, which now hangs at Blair Castle, shows Mary side by side with her son James VI. He is aged about 16 and she looks about 40, which corresponds with the painted date, 1583. However, this scene cannot have been painted from life, for Mary last saw her son in April 1567, when he was only 10 months old. By the time this painting was made, she had been in captivity for 15 years.

The painting's origins are obscure, but it seems to have been produced to support Mary's campaign of 1581–2 to rule Scotland jointly with her son. However, this proposal never came to fruition and Mary remained a prisoner in England.

As a young man, entranced by the prospect of ruling both Scotland and England, James marginalised his mother, but in later life he worked to rehabilitate her memory.

1567 22 August	Aug - Sept	29 September	1568 23 March	2 May
Mary's half-brother Moray is declared regent.	**Bothwell escapes** to Norway via Orkney and Shetland.	**Failed attempt to capture Charles IX and Catherine de' Medici at Meaux**, France. The Huguenots capture several cities and march on Paris.	The **Peace of Longjumeau** ends the Second War of Religion in France. Substantial concessions are made to the Huguenots.	**Mary escapes** from Lochleven Castle.

1567

24 April

Dunbar Castle, East Lothian
A courtship in captivity

Returning from Stirling without her son, Mary experienced one of the most bizarre episodes of her extraordinary life. The events read almost like the plot of a Shakespeare comedy, with all the underlying darkness that implies.

Who but Bothwell would have the chutzpah to abduct the queen? He was an aristocratic ruffian, known for his swashbuckling irreverence. He was much given to challenging people to duels; he cursed without restraint and was known to have a vicious streak. He had blithely stolen £1,000 from his rival nobles the Lords of the Congregation in 1559. He had escaped from Edinburgh Castle, one of the nation's most secure strongholds, in 1562. And he had already put it about that he meant to step into Darnley's shoes. But this latest venture showed boldness bordering on recklessness. Nonetheless, it had the desired effect.

Mary had felt ill after leaving Stirling and spent the night at Linlithgow, resuming her journey back to Edinburgh on 24 April. She was crossing the River Almond at The Briggs, a few miles from Edinburgh, when Bothwell struck. He and his 800 followers surrounded the queen's party and he led her away to Dunbar, the castle he had been awarded less than two weeks previously. One can almost imagine him flinging the queen over his shoulder like a bag of oats, but she remained mounted on her horse.

How willing Mary was – or whether she knew of the 'abduction' in advance – is open to debate. It seems that some of her nobles were less surprised than they pretended, and she may have been too. Upon this question rests the interpretation of the sexual encounter that followed.

Mary's faithful retainer Sir James Melville, who went with her to Dunbar, wrote that Bothwell had 'ravished her and lain with her against her will'. But in the years that followed, there were many conflicting accounts of Mary's relationship with Bothwell, and hence with Darnley's murder. It was widely rumoured that they were already lovers. In any case, her compliance is difficult to rule out. What is certain is that they slept together, and it is likely that Mary fell pregnant at this point.

Bothwell pressed home his suit to marry her, using the bond signed at Ainslie's Tavern as leverage. It seems clear that she came round to the idea quite quickly, and was not eager to escape his clutches. When Bothwell hurried back to Edinburgh to arrange his divorce from Lady Jean Gordon (citing adultery with her maid), Mary failed to escape, though it seems likely she could have overruled Bothwell's instructions to his domestic staff. In the event she stayed at Dunbar for 12 days, and seems to have convinced herself she was in love with Bothwell.

BOTHWELL meeting the QUEEN, seizes and conducts her as his Prisoner to Dunbar

1   The ruins of Dunbar Castle, dramatically sited on a rocky promontory in the Firth of Forth.

2   A fanciful illustration of Mary's abduction by Bothwell, published around 1800.

3   A portrait of Mary in her mourning veil after the death of her first husband. She was similarly veiled when she married Bothwell.

4   Holyrood Palace, scene of Mary's second and third weddings, as depicted in 1647.

1567

15 May

Palace of Holyroodhouse, Edinburgh
Third time lucky?

On 6 May, Mary and Bothwell returned to Edinburgh together, and by now they were pledged to marry. The couple's entrance into the city was heralded by the castle cannons, but they received a muted welcome from those crowds that did gather.

At St Giles' Cathedral in Edinburgh, John Knox's deputy John Craig read the banns with reluctance and unconcealed disapproval. When Bothwell confronted him he refused to apologise; indeed he again censured the planned marriage from the pulpit on Sunday 11 May. Summoned before the privy council, he stood his ground. Bothwell threatened to lynch Craig himself, but violence was averted.

On Monday 12, Mary officially pardoned Bothwell for the 'abduction' and raised him to the dukedom of Orkney, rendering him eligible to marry her. Meanwhile, however, Bothwell's enemies had regrouped at Stirling, calling themselves the Confederate Lords. Morton and Argyll had now enlisted Mary's former allies Atholl and Mar: the latter had refused to release Prince James to Mary's custody. Their stated aim was to free Mary from Bothwell's tyranny, and they were recruiting an army in the name of Prince James.

Mary and Bothwell cannot have been oblivious to this threat as they took their marriage vows at Holyrood on the morning of Thursday 15 May.

They were married in a Protestant service in the great hall at Holyrood Palace, led by Adam Bothwell, Bishop of Orkney, a cousin of the groom.

This was no grand state occasion: there were very few attendees. However, Mary's flair for glamour proved undimmed. She wore a sumptuous dress of rich black velvet embellished with gold and silver thread, decorously paired with a white *deuil* or mourning veil, in honour of her late husband.

Darnley had been dead barely three months. In little more than a month, Mary would begin her long years in captivity.

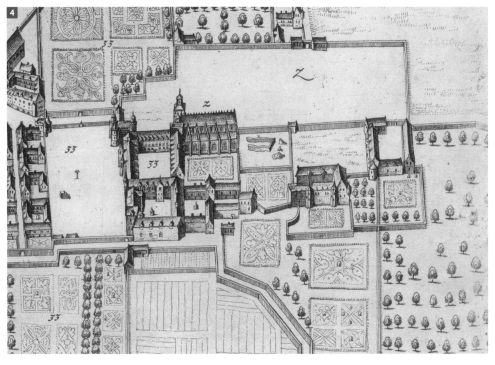

10 June

Borthwick Castle, Midlothian
Defiant to the last

15 June

Sir Simon Preston's House, Edinburgh
The caged bird

It was not a happy marriage. As early as her wedding day, Mary broke down to John Leslie, Bishop of Ross, telling him she regretted the whole thing. Even at the wedding dinner, a downbeat affair, she seemed stiff and listless. The following day she was heard calling for a knife with which to kill herself.

Bothwell's brutish side came to the fore, and he revealed a jealous streak. He forbade Mary to look at any other man, while he remained in contact with his hastily divorced wife, Jean Gordon. Belatedly, on 23 May, Mary staged a water pageant on the Firth of Forth and other festivities, but there was no masking her unhappiness.

Bothwell was also exhibiting unseemly arrogance and ambition. Like Darnley, he aspired to be named as king. He also began issuing legislation and had launched a presumptuous diplomatic correspondence with the English court.

None of this improved his popularity, and civil war was brewing. Mary's nobles had largely abandoned her to swell the ranks of the Confederate Lords. Maitland left, taking with him his wife, Mary Fleming, Mary's lifelong companion.

Over the past few months, Bothwell had been shrewdly gathering military resources. But while allied with him, Mary could no longer command the support of her nobles in raising an army.

Instead she had to fund it herself. She sold off gold and silver to be melted down into coin – even the gold font Elizabeth I had provided for James's baptism would have been melted if it were not too big.

On 6 June, Mary and Bothwell withdrew to Borthwick Castle, a fortified tower house 12 miles south-east of Edinburgh. Its massively thick walls, gunholes and lofty position made it highly defensible. But this did not deter attack.

Late at night on 10 June, a raiding party approached Borthwick, aiming to capture or kill Bothwell. He escaped via a postern (rear) gate and galloped to Haddington to raise troops. Left to hold the castle alone, Mary climbed to the battlements and bandied words with the raiders. Sir William Drury, deputy to the English ambassador, wrote of their 'divers undutiful and unseemly speeches used against their Queen and Sovereign, too evil and unseemly to be told, which, poor Princess, she did with her speech defend, wanting other means in her revenge'. Her speech did the trick, however, and the raiders withdrew to Dalkeith for the night.

The following day, Mary slipped out of the castle disguised as a page-boy, met up with Bothwell and went with him to Melrose to muster their forces. To this day, Borthwick Castle is said to be haunted by the ghost of Mary in boy's clothes.

The night of the Battle of Carberry (*right*) was Mary's last in Edinburgh, her first in captivity, and among the worst of her life. It was spent at a house owned by Sir Simon Preston, Provost of Edinburgh. Preston's main residence was Craigmillar Castle (see page 81), but when Mary appointed him provost in 1565, he rented a grand house on the High Street.

He was also landlord of the house where Mary was held, a short distance up the street. It stood directly opposite the Mercat Cross, on the site of the present City Chambers, where a brass plaque now commemorates it. The French ambassador du Croc, who witnessed the events, described the building as '*la principale maison de la ville*' (the town's main house). But it was by no means a royal residence.

After surrender at Carberry, Mary swore vengeance on the Confederate Lords, but she had no choice but to submit to them. Already dejected, she was shocked at the abuse heaped on her by their troops. 'Burn her!' they cried. 'Burn the whore! Kill her! Drown her!'

1 A print of Borthwick Castle by J.M.W. Turner

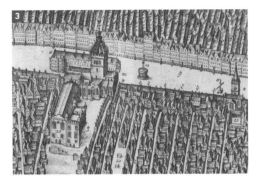

That long summer evening, she was led 'all disfigured with dust and tears' through the streets of Edinburgh, where further abuse was hurled at her by mobs primed by the lords. This must have been appalling for Mary, though it certainly did not represent the opinions of the populace at large.

She remained defiant throughout this mortifying ordeal, and is said to have refused food, demanding to be reunited with Bothwell. Her guards reportedly stayed inside her bedchamber, a great indignity which prevented her from undressing.

By morning, she was in a wretched state, though accounts vary over her conduct. John Beaton, her confidential agent in Edinburgh, described the events in a letter to his brother, the Archbishop of Glasgow. He wrote that she was repeatedly seen at her window, naked from the waist up, her hair dishevelled, begging her subjects for help.

In du Croc's account Mary is much more defiant. A third eyewitness reported, quite plausibly, that a large, supportive crowd gathered but was dispersed by a placatory announcement from the lords.

That evening, Mary was transferred to Holyrood, led by a troop carrying a banner depicting the murdered Darnley. Again, she ran a gauntlet of abuse. Later, under cover of darkness, she was taken north to Lochleven. Her life as a prisoner had begun.

2 A pen and ink illustration by Sir David Allan shows Mary led through Edinburgh after surrender at Carberry.

3 Edinburgh's High Street in 1647. The house where Mary was held is the tall one opposite the Mercat Cross at the centre of this picture.

15 June 1567
The Battle of Carberry Hill

On 11 June, the Confederate Lords seized Edinburgh. They issued a denouncement of Bothwell, revoking the verdict that declared him innocent of Darnley's murder. Huntly, one of few lords still faithful to Mary, attempted to take back Edinburgh, but was lured into the castle and trapped there.

The Confederate Lords quickly set about raising an army in Prince James's name, offering a generous 20 shillings a month. For this, they had raided what remained of the royal coffers. Argyll, meanwhile, was recruiting Highlanders in his lands to the west and north. The lords' army eventually numbered about 3,000.

Mary called on her loyal subjects to muster on 15 June at Musselburgh, a few miles east of Edinburgh. She and Bothwell had assembled a force of about 2,600, supported by cannon from Dunbar Castle. They marched through East Lothian towards Edinburgh, resting at Seton on the night of 14 June.

On learning of Mary and Bothwell's advance, the Confederate Lords led their army east towards Musselburgh, under a banner showing Darnley's corpse. The two armies sighted each other early on the morning of Sunday 15 June at Carberry Hill, above Musselburgh. It was a bright midsummer day and already warm.

For three hours, neither army risked a charge. The French ambassador, du Croc, attempted negotiation, but the Earl of Morton, commanding the lords' army, was intransigent. If bloodshed was to be avoided, either Mary must abandon Bothwell, or Bothwell must fight in chivalric single combat. Bothwell scoffed, saying, with some truth, 'There is not a single one of them who would not gladly be in my place.'

He was not one to decline a duel, but Mary intervened. She invited the Confederate Lords to request a pardon. They refused. The stalemate continued. The day grew hotter. Mary's troops were exhausted and began to disperse.

In the early afternoon, Sir William Kirkcaldy of Grange approached the queen under a white flag. He again urged her to leave Bothwell, who responded by renewing the challenge of single combat. The lords proposed Kirkcaldy as their champion. Bothwell spurned this offer as beneath him. He would fight, he said, with Morton.

Advanced in years and out of shape, Morton was a soft target. Patrick, 6th Lord Lindsay volunteered himself as a proxy and Morton gratefully gave him his two-handed sword, a revered Douglas heirloom.

Lindsay and Bothwell were preparing for the fray when Mary stepped in again. Either she was squeamish to see Bothwell's blood spilled, or she knew that the duel would not resolve the conflict. With few options open to her, she surrendered. She agreed to a separation from Bothwell, on condition that she would be unharmed and he could go free. There was a tearful parting, but the physical contact was probably limited to Bothwell taking Mary's hand for a moment (though some accounts report a full embrace). Then, with a handful of followers, he galloped off towards Dunbar. Not a drop of blood had been shed.

It was exactly a month since Mary and Bothwell had married. She never saw him again.

▲ An eyewitness's sketch shows Mary's surrender and Bothwell's escape.

1567-8

Lochleven Castle, near Kinross
The prisoner

The stated aim of the Confederate Lords had been to 'liberate' Mary from the clutches of Bothwell. It soon became clear that her liberty did not feature in their plans. After being captured, abused, threatened, paraded through the streets and imprisoned, she cannot have harboured any expectation of respectful treatment.

In the early days of her captivity, Mary was repeatedly pressured to divorce Bothwell but steadfastly refused. In the words of Sir Nicholas Throckmorton, sent from England as a representative of Elizabeth I, 'by renouncing him, she should acknowledge herself to be with child of bastard and forfeit her honour'.

But with or without Bothwell, a liberated Mary would overthrow the lords' new-found authority. She would also insist on a parliamentary enquiry into Darnley's death, which could all too easily reveal their culpability. The solution to both problems lay in a simple strategy: she must be implicated in the murder. A great deal of ingenuity would be directed to this aim in the coming years. Meanwhile, she must be kept from public view, in case her protestations of innocence were believed. So she was whisked north to an isolated medieval stronghold.

Today, Lochleven Castle sits on a small island, but then the island was even smaller, barely extending beyond the castle's walls. (The loch was partially drained in 1828, exposing parts of the island that previously lay under water.)

It comprised one large tower house, one small circular tower, various outhouses and a garden, all enclosed within a curtain wall. This was to be Mary's home for almost a year.

Initially, she was not allowed her retinue of companions – only two chamber maids – nor even her beloved wardrobe. Worse still, her host-jailer was the unsympathetic Sir William Douglas, a cousin of the Earl of Morton. Sir William's mother, also resident at the castle, was Lady Margaret Erskine, a former mistress of James V and the mother of Mary's half-brother Moray. She even claimed to have secretly married the king, which would render Moray legitimate and therefore rightful monarch.

This idea achieved little currency, but there was a more realistic alternative. If the infant Prince James could be declared king, a regent would be required to govern during his childhood, and Moray would be a natural choice.

Faced with her predicament, Mary fell ill yet again: among other symptoms, her limbs swole and developed pustules. Despair and exhaustion must have been factors, but she was also pregnant. This was not to last: on or around 20 July she miscarried twins, probably conceived at Dunbar.

A few days later, as she lay recuperating, she received a visit from Patrick, Lord Lindsay, the man nominated to duel with Bothwell at Carberry. He brought papers from the Confederate Lords and urged her to sign them.

Their purpose was crushing: by signing, she would abdicate the throne in favour of Prince James and endorse her half-brother Moray as regent. She held out until Lindsay threatened her life, but ultimately signed, saying, 'When God shall set me at liberty again, I shall not abide these, for it is done against my will.'

On 29 July, James was hastily crowned at the Church of the Holy Rood in Stirling. Sir William Douglas tormented his guest by firing Lochleven's cannons in celebration.

Moray arrived in Scotland a fortnight later, after a few months lying low in France, and soon came to visit Mary at Lochleven. Their conversations lasted two days and began with mutual recriminations. Gradually, Moray persuaded the weakened Mary that she had been in error – he may even have threatened her with execution. Ultimately, he manipulated her so successfully that she fully endorsed his regency.

He was proclaimed regent a few days later, on 22 August, and soon set about pilfering Mary's remaining jewellery. He even sold her finest pearls to Elizabeth I (see page 42).

After these tumultuous events, life at Lochleven Castle fell into a routine. Mary was moved from the circular Glassin tower to the third floor of the tower house, where evidence still survives for a little oratory where she said her prayers.

What else did she do, during her captivity? Doubtless she brooded on the treachery of her brother and her other lords and dreamed of revenge.

1 Lochleven Castle

▶ A dramatic depiction of Mary's escape from Lochleven, published in 1812.

She engaged in feverish diplomacy with Elizabeth I, attempting to justify her marriage to Bothwell and denying his involvement in Darnley's murder. She sent similar representations to the French court. But neither England nor France took steps to free her.

She strolled around the castle's formal garden; she practised her embroidery; she played cards; when the opportunity arose she danced and played music. She also flirted with the few young men who crossed her path. The Earl of Ruthven, who had conducted her to Lochleven, was sent away after falling for her. Sir William Douglas's younger brother George was also smitten, and secretly swore to serve her.

And she hatched escape plans. On 25 March 1568, she managed to board a boat disguised as a washerwoman, but was betrayed by her unblemished queenly hands.

On 2 May, she tried a different disguise, exchanging clothes with her childhood friend Mary Seton, who had been allowed to join her on the island. A courageous young servant known as Little Willie Douglas was her chief accomplice. He stole the castle key and, having released Mary, locked the door from the outside, throwing the key into a cannon's mouth. He had sabotaged all the castle's boats but one, which he used to row her to the shore, where her admirer George Douglas was waiting with horses stolen from his brother. It was an escape plan notable for its daring and simplicity, and it had worked perfectly.

Mary was among the most marriageable women in Europe. She was powerful, wealthy, vivacious and charming. Her beauty was the stuff of legend – even if it was exaggerated by the courtly conventions of flattery.

Yet she fared remarkably poorly in the important field of husbands. So it is worth comparing the virtues and failings of her trio of spouses – all of whom died before her, and in nasty circumstances – and examining the credentials of other candidates for her hand.

The husbands

Francis, dauphin of France [1]
later King Francis II

Born 19 January 1544
Date of marriage 24 April 1558
Advantages Future king of France; fabulously wealthy and privileged; civilised and well educated
Drawbacks Arrogant and petulant; feeble and unhealthy; weak governance skills
Died Orléans, 5 December 1560, aged 16, from an ear or brain infection

Francis was puny, sickly and – by all accounts – an unattractive personality. Nonetheless, he seems to have had a cordial relationship with Mary, fostered over years together in the French royal nursery. She expressed great happiness in a letter to her mother on her wedding day. She and Francis failed to produce any offspring, but that does not prove there was no sexual relationship. He died before any real suspicions of infertility could be sewn.

Henry Stewart, Lord Darnley [2]
later Duke of Albany; King of Scotland

Born 7 December 1545
Date of marriage 29 July 1565
Advantages Direct descent from Henry VII, with a strong claim to the English throne; wealthy and privileged; civilised and well educated; tall and handsome
Drawbacks Arrogant and petulant; deceitful and ambitious; dissolute and licentious; infected with syphilis
Died Edinburgh, 10 February 1567, aged 21, strangled when he escaped being blown up

Darnley's good looks and urbane charm seem to have blinded Mary to his failings. He was a heavy drinker and sexually promiscuous, having probably contracted syphilis by the time of their courtship. He appeared to tailor his religious beliefs to maximise political advantage, attending John Knox's fiery sermons even as he paraded his Catholic credentials. His arrogance, ambition and petulance must have made him insufferable.

James Hepburn, 4th Earl of Bothwell [3]
later Duke of Orkney and Lord of Shetland

Born 1534
Date of marriage 15 May 1567
Advantages Swashbuckling courage and swagger; loyalty to Mary at a time when she was desperate for support
Drawbacks Violent temper; foul mouth; royal ambitions
Died Dragsholm, Denmark, 14 April 1578, aged 44, after a long and extremely harsh imprisonment

Bothwell must have been a charismatic individual, a flamboyant and irrepressible hellraiser with boundless courage and a knack for cheating death. But he was also coarse and aggressive, on one occasion inflicting fatal injuries on an elderly servant who had irked him, in full view of Mary. He was ruthless in pursuing his ambitions, but at the time when he courted Mary she was in sore need of an anchor, and Bothwell had been her most reliable support. Their marriage lasted only a month, but as early as her wedding day she was said to be expressing regret.

MEN AND MARRIAGES

The also-rans

James Hamilton
later 3rd Earl of Arran
1532/6 – 1609

Period of candidacy 1543–6; 1560–1
Advantages Third in line to the throne
Drawbacks Protestant; conspired
against Mary of Guise; mentally infirm

Regent Arran began trying to arrange a marriage
between Mary and his son almost as soon as she was
born. This suit was not abandoned until Mary's French
marriage was agreed in 1548, when Arran became
Duke of Châtelherault and his son inherited the
earldom. The 3rd Earl was sent to France as a
member of Mary's retinue. He later became
commander of the *garde écossais*, the Scottish
bodyguard to the French king.

The suit was revived on the death of Francis II in 1560.
By this time, Châtelherault had also attempted to marry
him to Elizabeth I. However, the 3rd Earl suffered wild
delusions and in 1562 he was declared insane.

Lord Robert Dudley
later Earl of Leicester 1532/3–88

Period of candidacy 1563–4
Advantages The approved choice
of Elizabeth I
Drawbacks Elizabeth's favourite;
didn't want to marry Mary

Dudley was Elizabeth's favourite, and eventually sat on
her privy council. He courted her ardently, which she
encouraged, yet she persistently refused to marry him.

In 1563, she proposed a marriage between Dudley
and Mary, partly to sideline Don Carlos, partly to
bolster Anglo-Scottish amity, and partly as a means of
controlling both parties, whom she wanted to live at
her court. She made Dudley Earl of Leicester in 1564
to improve his eligibility, and Mary indicated interest.

However Dudley was extremely reluctant and backed
Darnley as a candidate – which happened to coincide
with Mary's wishes.

Prince Edward of England
later King Edward VI
1537–53

Period of candidacy 1543
Advantages Heir to the English throne
Drawbacks A pawn for his father,
Henry VIII

Henry VIII and Regent Arran signed the Treaty of
Greenwich on 1 July 1543. One of its principal clauses
was the betrothal of five-year-old Edward to seven-
month-old Mary. Henry wanted his daughter-in-law
to be raised at the English court, but was thwarted by
Mary of Guise.

In December 1543, the Scottish parliament overthrew
the treaty, to Henry's fury. He sent his army into
Scotland to enact savage reprisals and attempt to
coerce a marriage: the Rough Wooing.

On Henry's death in January 1547 Edward became
king, aged nine. He died aged 15 and never married.

Henry, Duke of Anjou
later King Henry III of France 1551–89

Period of candidacy 1564
Advantages Heir to the French throne
(though not expected to succeed);
sporty and artistic
Drawbacks Sexually profligate

Adored by his mother Catherine de' Medici and loathed
by his elder brother Charles IX, Henry was the third son
of King Henry II, and the third to become king.

After the death of his eldest brother Francis II, his
mother Catherine proposed a double union to secure
Anglo-Scottish-French relations. Elizabeth (30) would
marry the new king, Charles IX (14), and Mary (21) wed
his younger brother Henry (13).

Elizabeth was flattered by the offer but thought it
impractical. Mary thought Henry, a mere younger
brother to the king, beneath her. Nonetheless, it was
to Henry that she wrote her last ever letter.

Charles, Prince of Asturias
better known as Don Carlos
1532/6 – 1609

Period of candidacy 1560; 1563
Advantages Heir to the Spanish throne
Drawbacks Mentally and physically
infirm; petulant and wilful

A match with the recently widowed Mary was proposed
by her Guise uncles in 1560, but Catherine de' Medici
blocked it. Mary herself revived the proposal in 1563.
The marriage would have bonded her to a powerful
Catholic empire and dynasty, which greatly alarmed
Protestants in Scotland and England. It was the subject
of a heated debate with John Knox and prompted
Elizabeth I to offer her favourite, Lord Robert Dudley.
It could hardly have been a happy union. Already
unstable, in 1562 Don Carlos had fallen down a flight
of stairs and his behaviour became even more erratic
and aggressive. In January 1568, Philip placed him in
solitary confinement, where he died six months later.

Thomas Howard, 4th Duke of Norfolk
1536–72

Period of candidacy 1569–71
Advantages Cousin of Elizabeth I;
rich and powerful; hostile to Cecil;
from Catholic stock
Drawbacks Involved in Ridolfi Plot

One of the primary judges at Mary's tribunal at York
in 1568, Norfolk disapproved of Cecil's handling of
it. He took a shine to Mary, and visited her at Bolton
Castle, the home of his sister, Lady Scrope.

Maitland suggested the marriage, seeing it as a way to
neutralise Mary. She was enthusiastic, hoping to regain
her freedom, perhaps genuinely falling for Norfolk.
She sent him passionate love letters, and sought a papal
annulment of her Protestant marriage to Bothwell.

In 1571, the Ridolfi Plot to capture Elizabeth and place
Mary and Norfolk on the English throne was exposed.
Norfolk was tried in May 1572 and sentenced to death.

1568

Last Gasp

Mary was elated by her escape from Lochleven Castle. She was also furious with her half-brother, the Earl of Moray, who had so heartlessly manipulated her during his visit of August 1567. She was determined to recover her crown, and to unleash her wrath on him.

There was still a great deal of support for the queen, especially in southern regions of the country, and a number of nobles were loyal to her. It proved relatively easy to enlist backing and before long she was riding at the head of a substantial army.

But fortune was not on her side. In the event, Mary's taste of freedom, however vigorously and courageously she embraced it, was all too brief. Her final fortnight in Scotland was to prove a brief interlude in a much longer period of captivity.

▶ Dundrennan Abbey in Dumfries and Galloway, where Mary spent her final hours on Scottish territory.

1 Hamilton coat of arms at Craignethan Castle near Lanark. The Hamiltons gave Mary much-needed support after her escape from Lochleven.

1568

10–11 May

Craignethan Castle, South Lanarkshire Revival

As soon as she reached the shores of Loch Leven, Mary was filled with energy. She was exhilarated to have outwitted her enemies and determined to recover her throne. By the night of 3 May she was at Niddry Castle in West Lothian, stronghold of George Seton, the loyal 7th Lord Seton.

After resting there, she rode west into what is now Lanarkshire, heartland of the powerful Hamiltons. The family headed by the Duke of Châtelherault had not always served her well, but now declared loyalty.

Mary based herself between two of the family's properties: Hamilton Castle and nearby Craignethan Castle. Hamilton Castle has disappeared, but Craignethan still stands. It was built in the 1530s by Sir James Hamilton of Finnart, chief architect of James V. Its defences were virtually impregnable. Bounded on three sides by the steep, craggy Nethan Gorge, its vulnerable west side was shielded by an enormous wall and a deep ditch.

After a week in Hamilton territory, Mary had built up an army of perhaps 6,000 men. Her supporters included the earls of Huntly, Herries and Maxwell, as well as nine bishops and 18 lairds.

She was also joined by the Earl of Argyll, a former member of the Confederate Lords, who switched sides, bringing thousands of followers. Mary gave him the title Lieutenant of the Kingdom and placed him in effective command of her army. This decision, though logical, was to prove a very unfortunate one.

1 James Hamilton, Duke of Châtelherault, the former Regent Arran, whose family supported Mary during her final days in Scotland.

13 May 1568
The Battle of Langside

By 13 May, Mary commanded an army significantly bigger than her brother's. But rather than tackle him immediately, she set out to establish a power base at Dumbarton Castle on the west coast, where French forces might perhaps be summoned to support her.

Leaving Hamilton, she took her army west, which meant passing through potentially hostile territory owned by the Earl of Lennox. It also involved skirting close to Langside, where Moray's army was encamped. The Hamilton element of her army seems to have found this too good an opportunity to miss. Confident of a victory thanks to superior numbers, the vanguard, led by Lord Claud Hamilton, thundered down Langside's narrow high street to attack. Hamilton's men soon found themselves under ambush by Sir William Kirkcaldy of Grange, whose troops were armed with pikes and hagbuts (muzzle-loaded portable firearms).

It was now that Argyll's support for Mary's cause proved so catastrophic. At the crucial moment when the vanguard should have been supported by his main force, he was suddenly stricken by a seizure. He was rendered incapable of commanding the army, and Lord Claud's men were left to their fate. It has been suggested that Argyll's 'seizure' was a ruse, and his sudden change of allegiance had been a deceit. He was, after all, a Protestant and a longstanding ally of Moray.

Whatever the true reason for Argyll's collapse, it fatally undermined Mary's army. After a conflict lasting only 45 minutes, 100 of her men had been killed and 300 taken prisoner, including the loyal Lord Seton and Sir James Hamilton. Mary was urged by Lord Herries to flee south into Galloway, a Catholic heartland where she could still command support. Whether through exhaustion, fear or despair, she had lost the will to fight on. She accept Herries' advice.

Against the odds, the battle had been an overwhelming success for Moray. According to some accounts, only one of his soldiers had been killed.

	1568 13 May	16 May	23 May
	At the **Battle of Langside,** Mary's troops are defeated by a confederacy of Scottish Protestants under her half-brother Moray.	**Mary flees** to England.	**The Eighty Years' War** breaks out between Catholic Spain and Protestant rebels in the Spanish-owned Netherlands.

1568

16 May

Dundrennan Abbey, Dumfries and Galloway
Flight paths

Mary fled as swiftly as she could, riding 60 miles through the night to reach Terregles Castle, near Dumfries, sometime on 14 May. Her feelings must have been an overpowering cocktail of fear, betrayal, disappointment and despair. If she fell into the lords' hands now, she could expect further imprisonment, and perhaps death. Almost worse than that, she had scented victory. How different things might have been, if the confrontation at Langside had been better managed!

Mary described this journey in vivid terms in a letter of 21 June to her uncle the Cardinal of Lorraine: 'I have suffered injuries, calumnies, prison, hunger, cold, heat, flight without knowing where to, 92 miles cross-country without stopping or dismounting, and had to sleep upon the hard ground and drink sour milk, and eat oatmeal without bread ...'

All this while, she must have been contemplating the possibility of regrouping her army and rallying against the lords, but at Terregles, she decided instead to throw herself on the mercy of Elizabeth I. Her expectation of support from her cousin was not unreasonable. The English queen had been appalled and furious at Mary's treatment, which she viewed as a dangerous violation of royal authority. She was sympathetic, despite the venomous interpretation of events being fed her by her close adviser William Cecil.

Under cover of darkness, on the night of 14 or 15 May, Mary rode the 30 miles to Dundrennan Abbey. This peaceful monastery of the Cistercian order occupies a fertile valley on the River Nith. Parts of the cloister survive in good condition, and it is clear from the ruins of the church that this was once a magnificent complex of buildings.

At the time of Mary's visit, the Reformation was bringing the monastic way of life to a close, but Dundrennan was in control of the Maxwell family, who were still Catholic, and, more importantly, were still loyal to the abdicated queen.

It is not clear whether Mary slept at Dundrennan, but she did sit down here to write to Elizabeth, pleading for help. In a bid to stir the English queen to action, she enclosed a ring Elizabeth had given her in 1563, as a token of their mutual loyalty and affection.

But Mary was too afraid of capture to await an answer. On the afternoon of 16 May, she boarded a fishing boat and crossed the Solway Firth – scene of that calamitous battle a fortnight before her birth. She landed near Workington in Cumbria in the early evening, set foot on English soil for the first time, and never saw Scotland again.

2 An artist's reconstruction of Dundrennan Abbey as a thriving monastery. After the Reformation of 1560, monasteries began to be closed, but Dundrennan enjoyed the protection of the Catholic Maxwell family.

In early summer 1567, a rumour began to circulate: the Confederate Lords had discovered letters written by Mary that implicated her in Darnley's murder. This now-legendary cache of documents came to be known as the Casket Letters. The story surrounding them is one of the great enigmas of Mary's life.

Even their origins are murky. When the Lords assembled parliament to present this new evidence, they claimed the Casket Letters had been found before the showdown at Carberry Hill, thus justifying their armed rising against the queen.

Later came a contradiction. The casket, they now claimed, had been discovered after Carberry, when Bothwell's servants slipped into Edinburgh Castle and retrieved a locked silver casket from his chambers. One of them was captured and tortured until he surrendered it. The box was forced open and found to contain 22 documents, all written in French. They comprised a dozen poems, two marriage contracts and eight letters.

All of the original documents have now been lost. They were in Morton's possession at the time of his execution in 1581, but vanished soon afterwards. They may have been destroyed on the orders of James VI, who by then wanted to protect his mother's reputation.

When the documents first emerged, copies of the original French were made, together with translations into English and Scots. Some of these do survive. They were examined, together with the originals, by Cecil, who also had the handwriting closely scrutinised.

The Casket Letters formed the centrepiece of the evidence examined by the commission of October to December 1568. If they were genuine, they could provide solid evidence for a murder conviction.

Yet none of the letters is signed, none is addressed by name, and only one is dated. There is also strong evidence that they were either forged or doctored.

The chief focus was on two letters – the so-called Glasgow Letters – said to have been written by Mary to Bothwell from Stablegreen, the Lennox residence where she persuaded Darnley to return to Edinburgh. Of these two, more presently.

Letters from an unhappy wife

Three of the letters refer to a troubled relationship. There is an impassioned plea from an ill-treated wife, who describes a macabre piece of jewellery she has commissioned for her husband, 'a sepulchre of hard stone coloured with black, sewn with tears and bones'. There is a warning to an unfaithful husband, and there is an appeal to him to place more trust in the loyal spouse he has been abusing. These may well be genuine letters from Mary, but earlier ones, written to Darnley, not Bothwell.

The abduction letters

Three other letters deal with Mary's 'abduction' by Bothwell and include perhaps the most flagrant evidence of doctoring. It is clear from reading them that they were written – again, probably by Mary – after the abduction. But Mary's enemies wanted to show that she had colluded with Bothwell. In his clerk's annotation on one letter, Cecil quietly changed 'after Stirling' to 'afore Stirling' – that single word radically altering its significance.

The other two letters in this group are very similar, the main difference being the way Huntly is referred to. Bothwell and Huntly had been close friends and brothers-in-law, but they fell out when Bothwell hastily divorced Huntly's sister, Lady Jean Gordon, to marry Mary.

THE CASKET LETTERS

1 A French silver casket, said to be the one in which the Casket Letters were found. It is thought to have been given to Mary by her first husband, Francis II.

Any negative references to Huntly could only date from after that time. If these letters were to prove Mary's collusion in the abduction, they needed to be earlier. This seems to have prompted some adjustment to the references to Huntly.

The poems

The poems are mainly sonnets – a 14-line verse-form widely used for love poetry in the 1500s. These could have been written by Mary, but they might easily have been addressed to Darnley rather than Bothwell. They might even have been devotional poems addressed to God. However, they were presented by the Lords as further evidence of Mary's adultery with Bothwell.

The marriage contracts

The two marriage contracts certainly confirmed Mary's intention to marry Bothwell, but this was not in question. She had indeed signed such a contract on 14 May 1567. The point here was to show that they had agreed to marry weeks earlier. One contract is dated 5 April, but this must be a forgery since it refers to the Ainslie's Tavern bond, by which Bothwell tried to enlist support for his marriage to Mary. But this did not exist until 19 April. The other has a signature purporting to be Mary's, but its content dates it to after Bothwell's divorce.

The Glasgow Letters

The Short Glasgow Letter is the only one that indicates its date and place of origin: 'From Glasgow, this Saturday morning'. This would have to be 25 January, the only Saturday during Mary's visit. But even this is problematic. The letter speaks of the writer's impatience for the return of her lover. But Mary must have known that Bothwell had just left for the Borders. He could not have been expected back imminently.

The letter refers to bringing 'the man' to Craigmillar on Monday. This was what Mary had intended to do with Darnley, but the murder conspiracy needed him to be at Kirk o' Field, not Craigmillar. The writer also says that the man is 'the merriest that you ever saw', an unlikely description for the syphilitic Darnley.

The Long Glasgow Letter is the longest document found in the casket, and the most potentially incriminating. It goes into some detail about the writer's activities in Glasgow, her dealings with her ailing husband, her love for the man she is addressing, and apparently trivial details such as a nosebleed suffered by Darnley's father, and a bracelet she is making for her beloved.

There are passages in the Long Glasgow Letter that can be read as allusions to a murder plot – including one reference that suggests a plan to poison the victim at Craigmillar. Towards the end, the writer commands the reader to 'burn this letter, for it is too dangerous'.

But the letter's tone is patchy and uneven, with curious gaps and sudden switches of tempo and mood. Parts of it do ring true, but other passages are highly suspect, including annotations added at the end, referring to Bothwell and 'the Lodging in Edinburgh'. The Lords claimed this was a reference to Kirk o' Field, but it stands alone, without explanation.

Passing judgement

Most of the documents found in the casket are innocuous if viewed in isolation. Taken together, they would be highly incriminating, were it not for the many obvious inconsistencies. Their authenticity is highly dubious. But if the Confederate Lords were willing to falsify the evidence in this way, why were they not more thorough? Why do so few names appear on the documents; why was the dating so clumsily misjudged; why are there so few specifics?

When the scholar George Buchanan compiled the lords' evidence, he completely failed to mention the reference to poison. This strongly suggests it was inserted later, when the Lords altered the charges against Mary to include attempted poisoning.

It seems implausible that such a crudely uneven bundle of evidence was a careful forgery, created from scratch. A more likely explanation is that much of the material was genuinely written by Mary – and thus survived the scrutiny of Cecil's handwriting experts – but was taken out of its original context, re-ordered and amended as required. The outcome does not bear up to close examination, and it failed to convince the commission of December 1568.

Mary was not convicted, but nor was she exonerated. Cecil knew the evidence was tainted – he himself had tampered with it. For him, this was merely a frustrating setback. He would not rest until he had secured a conviction.

1

1568–87

A Long Decline

Mary spent more than 19 years in captivity – nearly half her life. Most of this time was spent in England.

The English authorities moved her from one residence to another, to keep her securely imprisoned, away from population centres where she might become a focus for dissent. Most of her jailers accorded her the comforts and respect appropriate to her status, but she never lost a burning sense of injustice. Her health worsened steadily during her imprisonment.

Meanwhile, William Cecil worked tirelessly to bring about her downfall. He was assisted in Scotland by the Protestant lords, and by George Buchanan, the poet and scholar, who assembled the evidence. He had been a favoured courtier, tutoring Mary in poetry and composing masques. But he was a fervent Protestant and his chief loyalty was to Darnley's family, who were hungry for revenge.

Among the evidence brought against Mary were the Casket Letters. These documents first appeared in 1567, and their authenticity was long debated.

Support for Mary was still widespread in Scotland. It came to a head in 1571, when Sir William Kirkcaldy of Grange led a rebellion against the new regent, Darnley's father. Kirkcaldy had fought for the Confederate Lords, but after Moray's death he took Mary's side. He now held Edinburgh Castle on her behalf, resulting in the Lang Siege of 1571–3, which ended with his surrender and execution.

Mary never was convicted for Darnley's murder. Her final downfall arose from the woeful Babington Plot against Elizabeth, to which she had subscribed, more in desperation than in hope.

She ended her days at Fotheringhay Castle. It is a poetic irony that only vestigial ruins remain of this grand royal residence; whereas Mary remains a legendary figure, fêted long after her death, despite the failings of her life and reign.

▲ Bolton Castle in North Yorkshire, one of Mary's earliest places of imprisonment.

▼ The site of Fotheringhay Castle, where Mary was tried and executed in 1587.

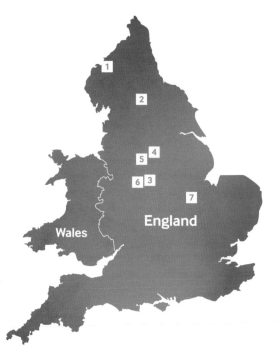

1 Carlisle Castle
2 Bolton Castle
3 Tutbury Castle
4 Sheffield Castle
5 Buxton Spa
6 Chartley Castle
7 Fotheringhay Castle

1568

28 May
Carlisle Castle, Cumbria
An own goal?

1 Carlisle Castle. The cannon on the battlements emphasise its longstanding role as a heavily defended border stronghold.

Mary's options after Langside may have been limited, but the decision to cross the border soon proved to be a mistake. Queen Elizabeth was highly sympathetic towards her cousin, and furious with Moray. But she was reluctant to embrace Mary while accusations of involvement in Darnley's murder clung to her. It was also feared that her presence might galvanise the predominantly Catholic north of England to rebellion. (The Rising of the North did in fact occur the following year, but was soon suppressed.)

However, Elizabeth's close adviser William Cecil – who had long regarded Mary as a profound threat – was delighted by this turn of events. He wasted no time in having her conducted to Carlisle Castle, a medieval stronghold repeatedly fortified over centuries of border warfare. Cecil sent the treasurer of the queen's chamber, Sir Francis Knollys, to supervise her imprisonment, together with the local magnate Henry, 9th Baron Scrope.

Mary repeatedly requested a meeting with Elizabeth, and it fell to Knollys to convey the English queen's evasive answers, emphasising to Mary that she was still under suspicion over the murder. He corresponded regularly with Cecil, discussing the fine details of her captivity. Her overriding mood comes over clearly in one letter: 'She showeth a great desire to be avenged of her enemies ... For victory's sake, pain and peril seemeth pleasant unto her, and in respect of victory, wealth and all things seemeth to her contemptuous [sic] and vile.'

She did not live frugally in captivity. Knollys was obliged to send for her dresses from Lochleven and Edinburgh. Gradually, her household of attendants grew to over 100, 'whereof,' noted Knollys, 'there be gentlemen, sewers, carvers, and cupbearers half a dozen, and as many gentlemen waiters ... cooks and scullions, and varlets of the chamber and lackies.' Mary was required to reduce her staff on several occasions, but it kept creeping up in number.

Mary Seton served as Mary's hairdresser. She was the only one of her Four Maries to remain with her throughout most of her long imprisonment, finally retiring to a convent in 1585.

In another letter, Knollys described a football match, one of the earliest recorded references to the beautiful game:

'Yesterday, her grace went out at a postern, to walk on the playing green ... About 20 of her retinue played at football before her the space of two hours, very strongly, nimbly, and skilfully, without any foul play offered, the smallness of their ball occasioning their fair play.'

However, she was closely watched by armed guards during these forays. An escape attempt was constantly feared.

Two queens in one isle

Mary and Elizabeth never met, though their meeting has often been imagined, for example by the German dramatist Friedrich Schiller in his 1800 play *Maria Stuart*. They had planned to meet in 1562 and exchanged a warm correspondence, partly in verses written in Italian and French, which both spoke fluently. A meeting in York was agreed, but then cancelled by Elizabeth following the outbreak of sectarian wars in France, and an attack of smallpox.

Although expressions of affection passed between the two thereafter, and Elizabeth always respected Mary as a fellow monarch, their diplomatic relations were often troubled and sometimes calculating and deceitful. Both queens were in Staffordshire in July and August 1575, but Elizabeth declined the opportunity to meet her deposed cousin.

1568 19 May	1569 November	13 December	1570 23 January	25 February
Elizabeth I has Mary placed in custody at Carlisle Castle.	**The Rising of the North** – a Catholic attempt to oust Elizabeth in favour of Mary.	**Northern rebels defeated.** Over 600 are executed in reprisals.	**Regent Moray** is shot and killed in Linlithgow.	**Pope Pius V** excommunicates Elizabeth I and anyone loyal to her. For Catholics, this makes Mary rightful Queen of England.

1568

8 December

Bolton Castle, North Yorkshire
Creature comforts

1569

4 February

Tutbury Castle, Staffordshire
A special guest

On 13 July, Mary was moved from Carlisle to Bolton Castle in Wensleydale, the seat of her custodian, Lord Scrope. It was the first of many moves that kept her out of the public eye and helped deter rescue attempts.

Bolton Castle was a more commodious residence than most of Mary's prisons: it was equipped with one of Britain's earliest central-heating systems. Mary occupied Scrope's own chambers in the south-west tower, and spent much of her time with his wife, Lady Margaret Scrope. She was a Catholic and shared Mary's growing hatred for her brother, now Regent Moray. (Lady Scrope's brother, Thomas Howard, 4th Duke of Norfolk, would later become one of Mary's suitors, embroiled in the Ridolfi Plot.)

Despite pleasant surroundings and convivial company, Mary's 26th birthday – her second in captivity – cannot have been a happy one. In Scotland, Buchanan had completed and circulated his vindictive dossier, which purported to prove her involvement in Darnley's murder. In York, a hearing in October had picked over the evidence, though the English lords (among them Norfolk) found it inconclusive. Now, at a reconvened hearing in London (although she probably did not know yet), Cecil had just taken delivery of the Casket Letters – the key documents 'linking' her to the crime.

In any case, she was not to be allowed to settle here for long. In the grim chill of late January, she was taken on a 10-day journey south, to Tutbury Castle in Staffordshire.

Arriving at Tutbury Castle in winter must have been highly dispiriting. A former hunting lodge on the site of a much earlier motte and bailey castle, it was cold, smelly, damp and – according to a survey of 1562 – 'decayed in many places'.

Mary's new host was George Talbot, 6th Earl of Shrewsbury, a rich and powerful nobleman in whose charge she would spend the next 14 years. One of her chief companions was the earl's wife, the notorious Bess of Hardwick. The couple had been married for just two years and were already at loggerheads, though Mary seems to have found common ground with both of them.

Shrewsbury was considerate in his dealings with Mary, though he was careful to stay aloof from any emotional engagement, despite persistent rumours of an affair.

2   Tutbury Castle, Mary's least comfortable place of confinement.

3   Bess of Hardwick and her husband the Earl of Shrewsbury, Mary's custodians for most of her imprisonment in England.

He ensured she was accommodated in considerable luxury, and went to some pains to secure permission for her to stay at some of his more comfortable residences – including Wingfield Manor and Sheffield Castle – and Bess's mansion at Chatsworth.

As for Bess, she had an astringent, ambitious character and a colourful history. She had served as a lady-in-waiting to Elizabeth I; had been imprisoned for seven months in the Tower of London and was now on her fourth marriage, with six living children. She would later marry her daughter Elizabeth to Charles Stewart, younger brother of Darnley and a claimant to the English throne.

Bess and Mary spent many hours together, and indulged in a shared passion for embroidery. The fruits of their elaborate needlework still survive.

Mary ate extremely well, sampling at will from 32 different dishes at every meal, leaving Shrewsbury considerably out of pocket. Not surprisingly – particularly given her limited opportunities to exercise – she gained a good deal of weight over the years.

Later Visits

Mary was relieved to depart from Tutbury in May 1570, thanks to Shrewsbury's negotiations with Elizabeth I. But she was to return for 11 unhappy months in 1585.

1572

3 June
Sheffield Castle, South Yorkshire
Another one bites the dust

1 Thomas Howard, 4th Duke of Norfolk, whose plan to marry Mary led to his execution.

On 28 November 1570, Mary was transferred to Sheffield Castle in south Yorkshire. This was the chief seat and grandest residence of the Earl of Shrewsbury, and became her main home for the remainder of her long years with him.

During her time, he also upgraded nearby Sheffield Lodge, a grand former hunting lodge, where she spent time from April 1573 onwards. The castle was destroyed during the civil war of the 1640s, but the lodge still stands.

These might have been relatively happy days, but for two miseries. The first was illness. Mary's old afflictions returned to torment her, with complications brought on by various factors probably including lack of exercise, stress, overeating, age and the damp conditions at Tutbury. Among her symptoms were abdominal pain, constipation, wind, frequent vomiting, catarrh, headaches and swollen limbs. Conscious of her potential liability, Elizabeth instructed that two doctors were to be in constant attendance.

The second upset was the Ridolfi Plot. Roberto Ridolfi was a banker from Florence, involved in a conspiracy to restore Catholicism in England, but also secretly working for Sir Francis Walshingham, Elizabeth's secretary and spymaster.

Ridolfi's scheme was to arrange a marriage between Mary and the Duke of Norfolk, depose and perhaps kill Elizabeth, and crown them in her place. He had even managed to enlist the support of Philip II of Spain.

The plot was exposed in early September 1571 while Ridolfi was in Paris. There was not enough evidence to convict Mary, but Cecil decided he could blacken her name. He arranged to have George Buchanan's damning dossier published.

2 Sheffield Lodge, upgraded by Shrewsbury for Mary's benefit.

3 Philip II of Spain, a sponsor of the Ridolfi plot, whose threat to Protestant England ultimately led to war.

It emerged among Cecil's circles at the end of the year, under the inflammatory title, *A Detection of the doings of Mary Queen of Scots, touching the murder of her husband, and her conspiracy, adultery, and pretended marriage with the Earl of Bothwell.*

Norfolk, meanwhile, was arrested and imprisoned in the Tower of London. He was tried for high treason in January and executed on 2 June 1572. Mary and Norfolk had pursued an earnest, if formal, courtship, and she was prepared to have her marriage to Bothwell dissolved. When she heard of the duke's death, she broke down.

To Bess of Hardwick, Mary sobbed that she feared her own letters might have incriminated Norfolk. Bess's riposte was a swift, heartless put-down. Nothing Mary had written could have harmed him, she asserted, since he had been tried by a fair-minded body of lords – a body presided over by her husband Shrewsbury.

1570 11 July	1571 April	July	4 September	1572 23 August
Darnley's father the Earl of Lennox is elected regent.	Sir William Kirkcaldy of Grange, keeper of Edinburgh Castle, occupies Edinburgh on behalf of Mary.	Supporters of James VI garrison Holyrood to challenge Kirkcaldy of Grange.	Regent Lennox is killed at Stirling during a skirmish with the Earl of Huntly, loyal to Mary. He is succeeded by John Erskine, Earl of Mar.	The St Bartholomew's Day Massacre begins in Paris and later spreads. Thousands of Protestants are killed by mobs.

1573

22 August
Buxton Spa, Derbyshire
Water works

Mary found little relief for her poor health, but her spa visits seemed to help – and certainly lifted her spirits.

The healing powers of Buxton's hot springs had been recorded by the Romans. In 1572, a certain Dr Jones published a treatise extolling the health benefits of the 'Ancient Baths at Buckstones'. Mary either read it or knew of it, for she began to pester Shrewsbury to allow her to visit.

Shrewsbury finally yielded, and eventually built Mary a private lodge in the town. She first visited in August 1573 and found the baths much to her liking, staying for five weeks. She returned many times.

Spas had already become gathering places for the aristocracy, and allowed Mary access to a more sophisticated social life than she usually enjoyed.

But these social opportunities Mary so relished caused concern to Elizabeth and Cecil. The dread possibility that she could become a focus for popular support – or another Catholic rising – was never far from their minds.

Shrewsbury reassured them, but could not refrain from treating Mary with decency. In the end, after 14 years, he was released from his custodial duties.

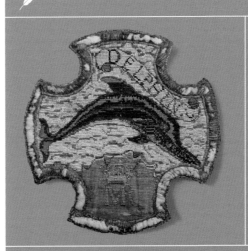

Puns and needles

Mary's love of needlework started as a child in France. When she was nine years old, woollen yarn was ordered so that she could begin her training under the supervision of Pierre Danjou, Henry II's personal embroiderer. She was encouraged in this by Catherine de' Medici, who was herself a skilled needlewoman.

Mary soon progressed to more complex embroidery and needlepoint. This was an approved activity for young ladies, but was also a way of providing personal gifts, and decoration for darkly-panelled palace rooms. Her training in France began a life-long pastime.

During her personal reign in Scotland, she would sew during privy council meetings, or while receiving ambassadors. However, it was in her long years of captivity, when physical exercise was limited, that Mary's love of embroidery really came to the fore. Aside from the activity itself, she greatly enjoyed devising what she was going to do.

During the Renaissance it was common for monarchs and nobles to adopt a pictorial emblem or *impresa*. Mary's mother, Mary of Guise, for example, had a phoenix as her emblem, with the motto '*En ma fin git ma commencement*', 'In my end lies my beginning'.

Mary delighted in these ciphers, which were treated as puzzles – displays of wit and intelligence.

For her own she chose the marigold, a plant which always turns to face the sun.

Her motto was '*Sa virtu m'atir*' ('Its virtue draws me'). An anagram of Marie Stuart, it was also a reference to the French writer Francis Rabelais' idea that education makes the young grow like plants in the sun. She accompanied this with her monogram – the letter M, both upright and reversed, so that it could be read either way.

While in the guardianship of the Earl of Shrewsbury, Mary spent long hours sewing with Bess of Hardwick and other companions. It is perhaps no wonder that the themes and puns of Mary's needlework often hinted at dynastic concerns. One panel she embroidered showed a dolphin leaping a crown (*above left*) – a reference to the dauphin, and therefore also to her own status. Another panel depicted a phoenix – the symbol of her mother, and therefore also a reminder of her Guise heritage. Her crowned cat with ginger curls, seen trapping a mouse (*above right*), was a pointed reference to Elizabeth I and herself.

Her output was remarkable, and it is astonishing how many pieces we have remaining from this period. Mary's embroideries are a physical glimpse into her thoughts, feelings and, indeed, amusements, during the last years of her life.

1572 28 October
Regent Mar dies after a short illness. He is succeeded by James Douglas, 4th Earl of Morton.

1573 17 May
The siege of Edinburgh Castle is brought to an end by a 12-day bombardment.

1574 30 May
Charles IX of France dies, and is succeeded by his brother Henry III.

1578 14 April
Bothwell dies at Dragsholm Castle, Denmark.

1579 September
James VI begins his personal rule in Scotland.

1586

18 July
Chartley Castle, Staffordshire
Written evidence

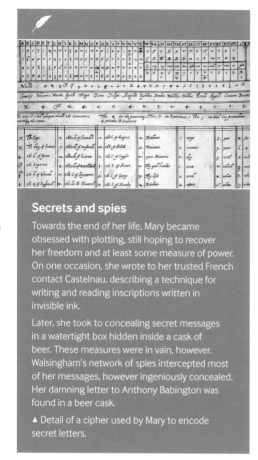

Secrets and spies

Towards the end of her life, Mary became obsessed with plotting, still hoping to recover her freedom and at least some measure of power. On one occasion, she wrote to her trusted French contact Castelnau, describing a technique for writing and reading inscriptions written in invisible ink.

Later, she took to concealing secret messages in a watertight box hidden inside a cask of beer. These measures were in vain, however. Walsingham's network of spies intercepted most of her messages, however ingeniously concealed. Her damning letter to Anthony Babington was found in a beer cask.

▲ Detail of a cipher used by Mary to encode secret letters.

In August 1584, a familiar figure reappeared in Mary's life. Her new custodian was Sir Ralph Sadler, who more than 40 years earlier, as Henry VIII's ambassador to Scotland, had reported her to be 'as goodly a child as I have seen'. Now aged 77, he had been assigned the unwelcome task of returning her to Tutbury and keeping her there.

Although he was loyal to Cecil, Sadler was too decent a man to treat Mary harshly. Her health was failing badly and she could barely walk, so he saw no harm in taking her hawking (under guard) – 'a pastime,' he noted, 'which she hath singular delight in'. When criticised for this lapse of discipline, he requested 'that some other had the charge'. He cannot have known he was exposing Mary to far worse.

Sir Amyas Paulet arrived at Tutbury around Easter 1585, and assumed control of Mary on 19 April. He was a staunch Calvinist, close to Cecil and Walsingham, and wasted no time in reining in her privileges and stepping up surveillance. He opened her mail, searched her private chambers and restricted her servants' contact with the outside world. Mary described him as 'one of the most zealous and pitiless men I have ever known'.

In a letter of 15 May 1585, she complained that he refused to allow her 'to send some trifling alms, according to my means, to the poor of this village; which, indeed I cannot but impute to very strange rigour, as it is a pious work, and one which no Christian can disapprove of'.

Cecil might justify Paulet's appointment by referring to the intrigues that had jeopardised England – and Elizabeth herself – in the early 1580s. In November 1583, Francis Throckmorton, nephew of Elizabeth's diplomat Sir Nicholas, was arrested. Under torture, he confessed to plotting with the Spanish ambassador Bernardino de Mendoza to facilitate a Catholic invasion of England and Scotland, led by the Guise family, with the support of Philip II of Spain and the Pope. Spies in the French embassy linked Mary with the plot.

In July 1584, the assassination of the Dutch Protestant leader William of Orange exacerbated anti-Catholic feeling among the Protestants of Europe. In October 1584, Cecil and Walsingham produced the 'Bond of Association'. This was framed as an oath of allegiance to Elizabeth and the Protestant faith, but it also provided for the summary execution of anyone threatening to harm her – or any 'pretended successor' who might benefit from such harm.

The bond could be read as a licence for Mary's assassination. In modified form, it was passed by Parliament in March 1585 as the Act for the Queen's Safety. This paved the way for Mary's prosecution.

Meanwhile, James VI had begun to assert himself. In November 1581, Mary had floated a proposal that she might reign jointly with her son, initially in Scotland, and in England too after Elizabeth's death. She sought French support for this idea, but in the end it was dashed by James himself. To her chagrin, he offered her the title Queen Mother, and nothing more.

1580 25 March	6 April	1581 2 June	1582 March	23 August	1583 July
Philip II of Spain becomes King of Portugal in the Iberian Union.	**The Dover Straits Earthquake** shakes southern England and northern France.	**James Douglas, Earl of Morton,** the former regent, is executed for complicity in Darnley's murder.	**The English Parliament** issues the Act against Reconciliation to Rome, levying fines against practising Catholics.	**Protestant nobles led by William Ruthven,** Earl of Gowrie, abduct James VI.	**James VI escapes** his captors and reaches his supporters at St Andrews Castle.

1 The effigy of Mary's elderly custodian Sir Ralph Sadler, on his tomb at Standon, Hertfordshire.

2 An illustration of the early 1600s shows Babington with his 'complices' and (in the background) their ultimate fate.

On 22 August 1582, after a flirtation with Catholic influences, the teenage king was abducted by the Protestant 'Lords Enterprisers' and held captive, initially at Ruthven Castle (now Huntingtower Castle) near Perth. The lords established a regime and received some support from Elizabeth. However, in June 1583 James escaped. Now 17, he declared his minority was over: he was ready to begin his personal reign. When James signed the Treaty of Berwick with England in 1586, Mary was completely sidelined.

Against this background, her involvement in the reckless Babington Plot is easier to comprehend. Sir Anthony Babington was a Catholic gentleman who had known Mary when employed by Shrewsbury at Sheffield.

In summer 1586, he and his comrades devised an all-but-unworkable plot to kill Elizabeth and enthrone Mary, with Spanish assistance. On 6 July he wrote a coded letter to Mary, seeking approval. This was swiftly intercepted and deciphered. It was then forwarded, unmarked, to Mary at Chartley, where she had been held since Christmas 1585.

Mary deliberated giddily for a week before taking the plunge. In truth, she had little to lose. Her reply of 18 July is cautious in tone, but its import was to prove undeniable:

'The affairs being thus prepared, and forces in readiness, both without and within the realm, then shall it be time to set the gentlemen on work; taking good order, upon the accomplishment of their discharges.

I may be suddenly transported out of this place, and meet without tarrying for the arrival of the foreign aid'.

Walshingham's spies added a postscript, hoping to fool Babington into identifying his comrades. He smelled a rat and fled, but was soon captured. He offered Elizabeth £1,000 to spare his life, but to no avail. He and his co-conspirators were hanged, drawn and quartered on 20 September.

Meanwhile, on 11 August, Mary was invited on a hunting trip by Paulet. It was a trick. She was apprehended and taken under armed guard to Tixall, three miles from Chartley. While she was held there, her chambers were ransacked and her papers were seized. The evidence was now in the hands of her enemies.

1584 May	July	1585 March	March	19 April
The Earl of Gowrie is executed.	**Francis Throckmorton** is executed for conspiring against Elizabeth I.	**The Act for the Queen's Safety** declares anyone benefitting from a plot against the queen guilty of treason.	**James** writes to his mother, declaring her Queen Mother and nothing more. She reacts angrily.	**The puritan Sir Amyas Paulet** replaces Sir Ralph Sadler as Mary's custodian.

1586

Fotheringhay Castle, Northamptonshire
Endgame

Mary arrived at Fotheringhay, her final destination, on 25 September 1586. She was in poor health and the journey had taken four days. Fotheringhay had been a splendid residence of Henry VIII, but since his death had been used mainly as a state prison. It was dilapidated but fairly comfortable. Crucially, it was within striking distance of London, but remote enough to be secure.

Cecil had prepared carefully. He had spent decades anticipating this scenario and failure now was unimaginable. The trial was to be held in Henry's former presence chamber. A throne was installed for Elizabeth, which represented her presence though she did not attend. Mary was allocated a high-backed chair with a red cushion. Chairs were still rare at this time: the judging commission of 30 or so magistrates and nobles sat on benches.

Mary at first refused to appear, on the grounds that no queen was answerable to foreign subjects. Cecil coldly informed her that there were legal grounds to convict her in her absence and eventually she complied, provided her protest was formally acknowledged. The trial began on 14 October.

Mary was defiant, denying any contact with Babington and challenging her prosecutors to produce anything she had written to him. But Walsingham had far more evidence than she realised.

Her original letter of 18 July had been destroyed by Babington, but not before it had been deciphered and copied. The copy was then re-encoded to produce a replica of the original. On seeing it, Mary's secretaries had confessed everything. Mary was shocked to tears.

Without legal representation, she fought her corner hard, attempting to discredit the evidence on the flimsiest grounds. Eventually she maintained that as a queen she was entitled to enlist foreign military assistance to free herself from wrongful imprisonment. But the weight of evidence bore down on her and eventually she lost heart. At the end of the hearing, she demanded an audience with Elizabeth, but this was not granted.

Cecil reconvened the commission on 25 October in the Palace of Westminster, London, while Mary remained at Fotheringhay. A guilty verdict was passed. Cecil cited the Act for the Queen's Safety and moved for the death penalty. Elizabeth baulked. She was resigned to Mary's death but very reluctant to see a fellow monarch subdued to the will of parliament. She would have preferred to see Mary quietly murdered by someone who had signed the Bond of Association.

The verdict was made public on 4 December. For nearly two months, Cecil campaigned for a death warrant. Elizabeth eventually signed on 1 February 1587, but secretly sent word to Amyas Paulet to murder Mary himself.

1586 6 July	4 August	20 September	11 October	4 December
The Treaty of Berwick, between Elizabeth I and James VI pledges mutual military support.	**The Babington Plot** is uncovered and Mary is implicated.	**Fourteen men are hanged, drawn and quartered** in London for their part in the Babington Plot.	**Commissioners arrive** at Fotheringhay Castle for Mary's trial.	**Mary is publically declared guilty** of conspiring against the life of Elizabeth I.

1 Mary's last ever letter, addressed to her brother-in-law, Henry III of France.

2 An eyewitness's illustration of Mary's trial, with Elizabeth's vacant throne top centre and Mary's chair top right.

◄ Sir William Cecil in old age. His lifelong goal of Mary's conviction was finally fulfilled at Fotheringhay.

Even Paulet was horrified. 'My good livings and life are at her majesty's disposition,' he wrote, 'but God forbid that I should make so foul a shipwreck of my conscience, or leave so great a blot to my poor posterity.'

Meanwhile, Cecil hurriedly assembled the privy council, who agreed to send the death warrant to Fotheringhay without Elizabeth's knowledge. Even this worked to her advantage, as it helped distance her from the deed.

On 7 February, Mary was in good spirits at Fotheringhay when her former host the Earl of Shrewsbury arrived, accompanied by the Earl of Kent. They had been charged with managing her execution. They told her she would die the following morning.

She responded with dignity: 'You will do me a great good in withdrawing me from this world, out of which I am very glad to go.' She also declared herself a Catholic martyr, one of the key themes of her final days, and one Elizabeth had been keen to suppress.

She prayed, made provision for her retinue to receive pensions, divided up her remaining belongings, then sat at her writing table. The last of her thousands of letters was addressed to Henry III of France, younger brother of her former husband Francis, whom she had known since childhood. 'It remains for me to beg Your Most Christian Majesty, my brother-in-law and old ally, who have always protested your love for me, to give proof now of your goodness ... by having prayers offered to God for a queen who has borne the title Most Christian, and who dies a Catholic, stripped of all her possessions.'

8 February

Fotheringhay Castle, Northamptonshire
Checkmate

The following morning, Mary rose at 6am to prepare herself. She wore black outer clothing, with a white veil and cap and a crimson bodice. Her rosary beads were strung at her waist. About two hours later, there was knocking at her door. Clutching her crucifix and prayer book, she made her way purposefully to the castle's great hall, accompanied by Shrewsbury, Kent and the local sheriff.

Outside the hall, she instructed her staff, 'Tell my friends that I die a true woman to my religion, and like a true Scottish woman and a true French woman.' She insisted that they would accompany her to the platform on which the executioner, Bull, and his assistant were waiting.

With great composure, Mary sat on a stool and listened while her death sentence was read out. This was to be followed by a Protestant sermon delivered by Richard Fletcher, Dean of Peterborough. But Fletcher stumbled repeatedly over his speech until Mary interrupted, saying, 'Mr Dean, I will not hear you. You have nothing to do with me, nor I with you.'

An indignant Fletcher moved on to prayers, but Mary and her retinue spoke over him, saying their own Catholic prayers. She then kissed her crucifix and crossed herself, reasserting her Catholic martyrdom.

It was time to submit to the executioners, but as she disrobed, Mary had a surprise quite literally up her sleeves. Beneath her black clothes she was wearing an outfit of deep red: the Catholic colour of martyrdom. Thus clad, she knelt, reciting a Latin Psalm, and bared her neck for the headsman's blade.

And now came Bull's infamous botch job. His axe came down hard, not on Mary's neck but on the back of her head. There are conflicting reports on Mary's response, but she did not flinch. Even the second blow failed to sever her head completely, and a third was require to part it from her neck. It is said that Mary's lips continued to move for 15 minutes or more.

As Bull lifted the head, there was a further fumble: Mary had been wearing a wig. It parted from her grey-haired head, which tumbled to the stage, as if mocking the solemnity of the occasion.

And then, one last surprise: a little dog emerged wailing from its hiding place among its late mistress's skirts and could not be removed before it had become soaked in her blood. It remained the world's most famous Skye terrier until being supplanted by Greyfriars Bobby nearly 300 years later.

At last, Mary's struggles had been brought to an end.

1587 1 February	8 February
Elizabeth signs a warrant for Mary's execution.	**Mary is executed** at Fotheringhay Castle.

Epilogue

1 A wax death mask supposedly of Mary.

2 Mary's execution, in a Dutch illustration of about 1608.

3 Mary's state funeral at Peterborough in August 1568.

Mary's organs were removed and interred secretly at Fotheringhay. Her clothing and effects were burned or otherwise destroyed. The fear was that any vestige of her, any shred of clothing or smear of blood, might be treated as a relic and become a focus for insurrection. The rest of her body was not buried. It remained at Fotheringhay, embalmed and enclosed in a lead coffin.

Six months later, her remains were taken to Peterborough Cathedral, where a discreet state funeral was held – after dark, to avoid attracting major crowds.

Elizabeth I learned of Mary's execution the morning after it happened. Her fury that the death warrant had in fact been used turned quickly to sorrow and distress – though perhaps with an element of show. The contemporary historian William Camden recorded that, 'she gave herself over to grief, putting herself into mourning weeds and shedding abundance of tears'.

Her reign continued for a further 16 years, until her death on 24 March 1603. She was 69, had never married and left no children.

James VI was declared as Elizabeth's successor within hours. He left Scotland on 5 April 1603 to take up his new throne in London, promising he would visit his native land every three years. He returned only once, in 1617.

He was King of Scots for nearly 58 years, and of England for 22 of them – by far the longest reign of the enduring Stewart/Stuart dynasty.

In 1584, he had crushed Mary's hopes of ruling jointly, relegating her firmly to the role of Queen Mother. After his accession to the English throne, however, he sought to rehabilitate his late mother's reputation. He commissioned grand monumental tombs at Westminster Abbey for both Mary and Elizabeth, spending much more on Mary's than on Elizabeth's. In 1612 he had Mary's remains moved from Peterborough to Westminster.

Bothwell escaped Scotland via Shetland, with William Kirkcaldy of Grange in hot pursuit. Following a sea battle, his ship limped to the Norwegian coast, where he was arrested. He was taken to Bergen, where he ran into an old flame, Anna Trondsen, who sued him for breach of an earlier promise to marry her.

Thereafter, he became a political football, with England and Scotland seeking his extradition, and Denmark hoping to barter him for Orkney and Shetland. He was ultimately imprisoned at Dragsholm Castle in Zealand, where it is said he was kept chained to a post for years on end, living in his own filth. He died insane, on 14 April 1578.

Henry III of France was assassinated by a Catholic extremist in 1589, bringing the Valois dynasty to an end. He was succeeded by his cousin Henry IV, founder of the Bourbon dynasty. Ironically, the new king was a Protestant.

3

Sites directory

1 Alloa Tower
National Trust for Scotland
Alloa, Clackmannanshire
FK10 1PP
0844 493 2129
Admission charge
See page 77

2 Balvenie Castle
Castle Road, Dufftown
AB55 4GH
01340 820 121
Admission charge
See page 56

3 Beauly Priory
Beauly, Inverness-shire
IV4 7BX
See page 61

4 Borthwick Castle
In private ownership
The castle operated as a hotel for 40 years before closing in 2013.
North Middleton, Midlothian EH23 4QY
See page 94

5 Callendar House
Falkirk Community Trust
Callendar Park, Falkirk
FK1 1YR
01324 503 770
See page 68

6 Castle Campbell
Above Dollar, Clackmannanshire
FK14 7PP
01259 742408
Admission charge
See page 58

7 Craigmillar Castle
Craigmillar Castle Road, Edinburgh EH16 4SY
0131 661 4445
Admission charge
See page 81

8 Craignethan Castle
By Blackwood, Lanarkshire
ML11 9PL
01555 860 364
Admission charge
See page 102

9 Crichton Castle
By Pathhead, Midlothian
EH37 5XA
01875 320 017
Admission charge
See page 54

10 Dumbarton Castle
Castle Road, Dumbarton
G82 1JJ
01389 732 167
Admission charge
See page 23

11 Dunbar Castle
Vestigial ruins
The castle was 'cast doun' after Bothwell fled Scotland in 1567.
Dunbar, East Lothian, EH42 1EX
See pages 75 and 92

12 Dundrennan Abbey
By Kirkcudbright, Dumfries and Galloway DG6 4QH
0131 668 8800
Admission charge
See page 103

13 Edinburgh Castle
Castlehill, Edinburgh
EH1 2NG
0131 225 9846
Admission charge
See pages 48, 76 and 106

14 Edzell Castle
By Brechin, Angus
DD9 7UE
01356 648 631
Admission charge
See page 55

15 Falkland Palace
National Trust for Scotland
Falkland, near Cupar, Fife KY15 7BU
0844 493 2186
Admission charge
See page 14

16 Hermitage Castle
Near Newcastleton, Roxburghshire TD9 0LU
01387 376 222
Admission charge
See page 78

17 Palace of Holyroodhouse
The Royal Collection
Holyrood, Edinburgh
EH8 8DX
0131 556 5100
Admission charge
See pages 47, 67, 74 and 93

18 Huntingtower Castle
By Perth PH1 3JL
01738 627 231
Admission charge
See page 69

19 Inchmahome Priory
By Port of Menteith
FK8 3RA
01877 385 294
Admission charge
See page 22

20 Inverness Castle
In civic/local government use
Castle grounds accessible on foot. Vestiges of medieval fabric remain.
Castle Street, Inverness
IV2 3EG
See page 56

21 Kirk o'Field
Vanished
Now the site of Old College. South Bridge, Edinburgh
EH8 9YL
See page 88

22 Lamb's House
In private ownership
19 Water Street, Leith, Edinburgh EH6 6SU
Admission charge
See pages 46

23 Linlithgow Palace
Kirkgate, Linlithgow, West Lothian EH49 7AL
01506 842 896
Admission charge
See pages 12 and 92

24 Lochleven Castle
Access via Pier Road, Kinross KY13 8UF
01577 862 670
Admission charge
See page 96

25 Lochmaben Castle
Near Lochmaben on the B7020, Dumfries and Galloway, DG11 1LP
See page 8

26 Mary Queen of Scots House, Jedburgh
Scottish Borders Council
Open to the public as a museum.
Queen Street, Jedburgh, Scottish Borders TD8 6EN
01835 863 331
See page 79

27 Place of Stablegreen
Vanished
Now the site of Barony North Church.
Cathedral Square, Glasgow G4 0QY
See page 88

28 Sir Simon Preston's House
Vanished
Now the site of the City Chambers. A brass plaque commemorates the night Mary spent here as a prisoner.
253 High Street, Edinburgh EH1 1YJ
See page 94

29 Rossend Castle
In private ownership
Burntisland, Fife KY3 0DF
01592 873 535
Rossend's 16th-century painted ceiling is in the National Museum of Scotland, Chambers Street, Edinburgh EH1 1JF
See page 60

30 Spynie Palace
By Elgin, Moray IV30 8XJ
01343 546 358
Admission charge
See page 57

31 St Andrews Castle
The Scores, St Andrews, Fife KY16 9AR
01334 477 196
Admission charge
See pages 20 and 60

32 Stirling Castle
Castle Wynd, Stirling
FK8 1EJ
01786 450 000
Admission charge
See pages 18, 82 and 90

33 Tantallon Castle
By North Berwick, EH39 5PN
01620 892 727
Admission charge
See page 80

34 Traquair House
In private ownership
Open to the public
Innerleithen, Peeblesshire
EH44 6PW
01896 830 323
Admission charge
See page 77

35 Wemyss Castle
In private ownership
Gardens open to the public, weekdays May–July by arrangement only.
East Wemyss, Fife
KY1 4TE
01592 652 181
Admission charge
See page 66

36 Whithorn Priory
6 Bruce Street, Whithorn, Dumfries and Galloway
DG8 8PY
Admission charge
See page 61

A The Battle of Solway Moss, 1542
See page 14

B The Battle of Pinkie Cleugh, 1547
See page 21

C The Battle of Corrichie, 1562
See page 56

D The Battle of Carberry Hill, 1567
See page 95

E The Battle of Langside, 1568
See page 102

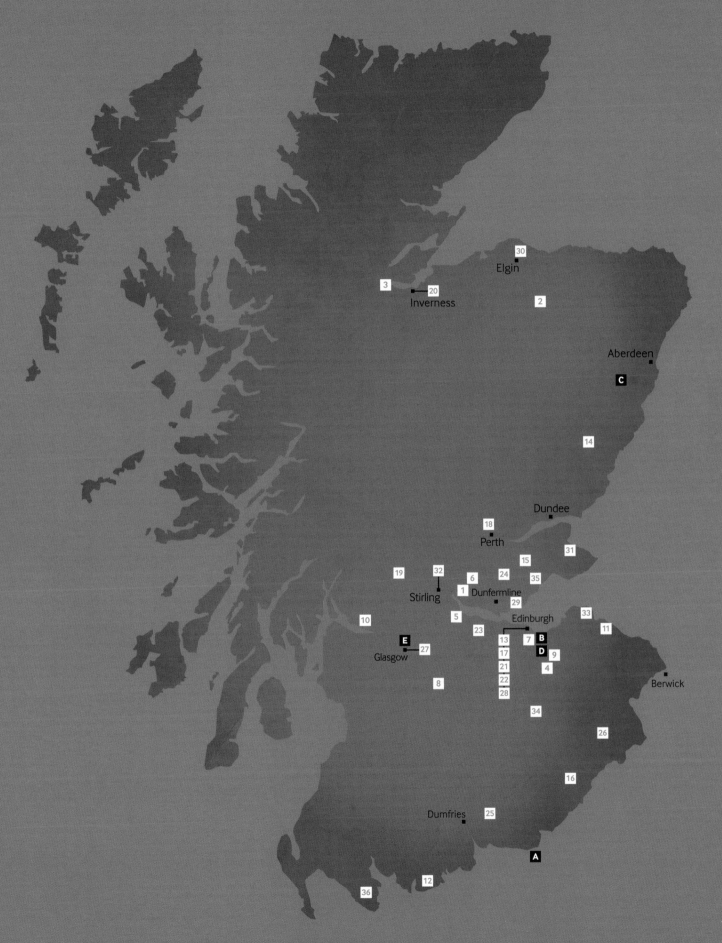

Elgin

30

Inverness
3 20

2

Aberdeen
C

14

Dundee

18
Perth

31

15

19 32
6 24 35

1 Dunfermline
Stirling 29

5
Edinburgh
33

10
23 11
E
27 13 7 B
Glasgow 17 D 9
21 4

22
8
28 Berwick

34

26

16

Dumfries 25

A

12

36

119

Bibliography

A wealth of material has been published on Mary Queen of Scots and the world she inhabited. The following publications are among those referred to in the preparation of this book.

J. Ashelford, *A Visual History of Costume: the Sixteenth Century* (1986)

C. Bingham, *Darnley: A Life of Henry Stuart, Lord Darnley, Consort of Mary Queen of Scots* (1995)

C. Bingham, *James V, King of Scots, 1512–1542* (1971)

D. Breeze, *A Queen's Progress* (1987)

G. Buchanan, *A Detection of the Actions of Mary Queen of Scots* (1571)

D.H. Caldwell and R.K. Marshall, *The Queen's World: A Celebration* (1987)

J. Cameron *James V: The Personal Rule, 1528–1542* (1998)

G. Dalgleish and R. Marshall (eds), *The Art of Jewellery in Scotland* (1991)

J. Dawson, *Scotland Reformed, 1488–1587* (2007)

H. Dingwall, *A History of Scottish Medicine: Themes and Influences* (2003)

H. Dingwall et al *Scottish Medicine: An Illustrated History* (2011)

A. Fraser, *Mary Queen of Scots* (1969)

E.M. Furgol, 'The Scottish itinerary of Mary Queen of Scots, 1542–8 and 1561–8' in *Proceedings of the Society of Antiquaries of Scotland*, vol 117 (1987)

J. Guy, *My Heart is My Own: The Life of Mary Queen of Scots* (2004)

S. Harris, 'Mary, Queen of Scots and Sir Simon Preston's House' (1983)

D. Hay Fleming, *Mary Queen of Scots from her Birth to her Flight into England* (1897)

J. Knox, *The History of the Reformation of Religion in Scotland* (1586–7)

A. Labanoff, *Lettres Inédites de Marie Stuart* (1839)

R. Lindsay of Pitscottie, *The History and Chronicles of Scotland* (1728)

R.H. Mahon, *The Tragedy of Kirk o'Fields* (1930)

R. Marshall, *Costume in Scottish Portraits 1560–1830* (1986)

Z. Oddy, *Mary, Queen of Scots' House, Jedburgh* (2004)

M. Merriman, *The Rough Wooings: Mary Queen of Scots 1542–51* (2000)

The Register of the Privy Council of Scotland (1545–1689)

P.A. Ritchie, *Mary of Guise in Scotland, 1548–1560* (2002)

J. Sadler, *Scottish Battles* (1996)

H. Smailes, *The Queen's Image: A Celebration of Mary, Queen of Scots* (1987)

D. and J. Steel, *Mary Stuart's Scotland* (1987)

M. Swain, *The Needlework of Mary Queen of Scots* (1986)

S. Watkins, *Mary Queen of Scots* (2001)

A. Weir, *Mary Queen of Scots and the Murder of Darnley* (2003)

J. Wormald, *Mary Queen of Scots: A Study in Failure* (1988)

Credits

First published by Historic Scotland 2013
Printed from sustainable materials 2019
© Historic Environment Scotland 2019
ISBN 978 1 84917 130 4

Historic Environment Scotland
Scottish Charity No. SC045925

Principal Office
Longmore House, 1 Salisbury Place, Edinburgh EH9 1SH

Text Andrew Burnet, Dr Nicki Scott and Sally Gall
Design Stand Ltd
Photography Historic Scotland Photo Unit
Illustration p.13 Stephen Conlin/Pictu Ltd
Illustration p.18 David Lawrence
Illustration p.48 Brian Lee
Illustrations p.51 and **p.82** David Simon
Digital reconstruction p.103 Peter Lorimer/Pighill

Model Erin Smith
Hair Gordon Wilson

Our thanks are due to the wardrobe department of the Royal Lyceum Theatre Company